It's party time!

It's party time!

Fun ideas for children's parties

Fransie Snyman

M ETZ
PRESS

Published by Metz Press
Unit 106, Hoheizen Park 1, Hoheizen Avenue,
Hoheizen 7530 South Africa

First edition Struik Timmins 1990
This edition Metz Press 2002
Copyright © Metz Press
Text copyright © Fransie Snyman
Photographs © Metz Press

EDITOR	jack
COVER DESIGN	jack
BOOK DESIGN AND LAY-OUT	jack
PHOTOGRAPHS	David Pickett, Alchemy Foto Imaging cc
ILLUSTRATIONS	Karmien Kruth
PRODUCTION	Andrew de Kock
REPRODUCTION	Cape Imaging Bureau, Cape Town
PRINTING AND BINDING	Tien Wah Press, Singapore
ISBN	1-875001-66-2

Contents

Introduction

Children of all ages love attending parties and it's important that they remember your child's special day as a wonderful one. To ensure that the memory is a fond one for everyone, including yourself, it's essential to be well prepared. Expensive snacks and decorations seldom impress children, so don't waste your time! With this book I hope to inspire you and show you how to give a memorable party that is both inexpensive and hardly any trouble to yourself.

There are 12 party themes for one- to nine-year-olds and four themes for 10- to 12-year-olds. For each theme there are detailed instructions for the preparation of every aspect – invitations, decorations, snacks and dessert – as well as a template and instructions for a birthday cake in keeping with the theme.

The theme menu includes both savoury and sweet snacks making it easy to present an interesting variety without going overboard.

All the invitations and decorations, cakes, snacks and cool drinks presented in the book are easy to prepare and, because everything is so straightforward, your child can be involved in the arrangements and preparations right from the start.

The themes have been chosen not only for their popularity with children and mums alike, but also because they guarantee success time after time.

In this edition you will also find a section with tips and recipes for children with diabetes and/or one of the more general food allergies (see page 92).

IMPORTANT CONSIDERATIONS

WHEN AND WHAT TIME?

It would be best to have the party on the day of the birthday itself, but having the party the following weekend might be preferable if the party could interfere with homework or extra-mural activities.

The age of the birthday child and his or her guests will determine the starting time of the party, which in most cases should be kept to daytime.

WHERE?

The most obvious place is your own home or garden, but what if you stay in a flat without sufficient space, or would like to have the party outdoors?

There is bound to be a park nearby where there are swings and slides; set a table under a shady tree and perhaps have the help of other mums.

Another possibility for a party away from home is to take a picnic hamper to the nearest botanical garden, zoo, public pool or beach.

You could also try a combination of a meal at a restaurant and a visit to the children's theatre, the circus, the zoo or the cinema. Many playschools are willing to let out their premises over weekends, so do make enquiries at those nearest to you.

If you're willing to splash out, you could hire a marquee, a boathouse or a banquet hall and get a caterer to prepare all the food, but then, of course, you wouldn't be reading this book!

WHO AND HOW MANY?

This can be one of the trickiest decisions and your child will be only too pleased to help! Be firm if he wants to invite the whole class and you can only accommodate 10 friends.

The most important person to have at the party is your child's best friend, so ensure that invitations are sent out in good time (two weeks should be ample). If your child wants both boys and girls at the party, try to ensure that the sexes are balanced.

Cost and space will determine the number of guests, and here you'll have to be practical. Bear in mind that the amount of money you spend won't determine the success of the party and most importantly, the old saying 'the more the merrier' does not always hold true!

PLANNING THE PARTY

Once the number of guests, time and venue of the party have been set, the next step is to decide on a theme. List everything that will be required for the party, delete what you already have and buy the rest – don't forget film for your camera and ensure you have enough adhesive tape at home!

Most of the arrangements for a pre-teen party can be left to the youngsters themselves, with the understanding that you have the final approval.

Remember to book the magician, pony rides, videos and other entertainment well in advance to avoid disappointment.

Apart from the guests and a venue, a party requires invitations, decorations, snacks, drinks and entertainment, each of which should be planned separately.

INVITATIONS

Children love receiving invitations: it makes them feel important and creates a feeling of expectancy. It is unnecessary to buy expensive

invitations. Help your child to make his own cards, and if he can, write in the details. Decorate the invitation with a drawing or a cut out picture.

State what time the party will begin and when the friends should be collected.

Written invitations are preferable to oral ones, as they serve as a reminder of the party. Ask the friends to reply at least a week before the big day.

If the birthday child is old enough, encourage him or her to write thank you notes to those who attended the party.

Except for the pre-teen parties, each theme has suggestions for invitations that you and your child can make yourselves (see page 13), but stationers stock quite a variety if you don't have the time.

DECORATIONS

Decorating the house always adds to the party spirit. Stick a 'WELCOME TO THE PARTY!' poster on the front door, tie balloons and string streamers across the room to create a festive atmosphere.

Decorate the table with colourful serviettes, paper plates and cups. Individual place cards, in keeping with the theme of the party, can also be used as part of the decorations (see diagram to make easy place cards).

A brightly coloured plastic or paper tablecloth will add a cheerful note as well as make clearing up that much easier. Paper hats, crackers and blowers are essential

and have proved to be favourites with children of all ages.

It is a good idea to seat younger children around a table. They will have lots of fun looking for their names to see where they will be sitting.

Up to the age of nine each child should have his or her own plate filled with goodies; this avoids a wild rush with everyone scrambling to get something to eat. Of course, extra treats can be placed in bowls or plates on the table.

SNACKS

Always provide something savoury, something sweet, something soft, something hard and of course, something to take home. Preschoolers are often just as fond of savouries as adults are, so don't forget the cocktail sausages, cheese cubes, potato crisps and interesting sandwiches!

Most cakes are suitable for children's parties, but it's preferable to stick to simple sponge mixtures and to change the colouring and flavouring and/or bake them in different shapes to suit your theme.

No party would be complete without jelly and ice cream, which is just as well as it always looks festive. Ice cream is a firm favourite with all children and can be decorated in various ways to add interest. Jelly can be served in hollowed-out oranges, pretty glass bowls or brightly coloured plastic ones.

DRINKS

At a children's party, it's preferable to serve fruit juices, milkshakes or punch instead of fizzy drinks. Serve them in brightly coloured plastic or paper cups, with straws decorated with ribbon or streamers. Juice lollipops can be made by pouring juice into moulds, inserting sticks and freezing them.

You certainly do not wish to see your best glasses broken and possibly injuring one of the children. So stick to paper and plastic cups and rather put away your glasses.

GAMES & ENTERTAINMENT

At the back of the book, games for the various age groups are discussed (see page 80). These are the cheapest form of entertainment and are great fun if sufficient space is available.

Indoor games, however, should test children's mental rather than physical abilities. Ensure that they

also play some non-competitive games and that everyone gets involved.

Other forms of home entertainment for younger children are videos, pony rides (if you have the space), magicians or puppet shows – remember to book these early to avoid disappointment.

Card games, Scrabble or music videos are popular with older children. They will probably also want to dance, so ensure that there is enough space and ask everyone to bring along their favourite CD.

SUGGESTIONS FOR VARIOUS AGE GROUPS

ONE TO TWO

Parties for one-to two-year-olds are really for the mums, as they have to be present to keep an eye on their offspring.

At this age toddlers are far too young to enjoy a party and hardly understand what is happening anyway. For a first birthday party it might be a better idea to invite grannies and grandpas and other relatives.

A two year-old's party could include a few friends – but bear in mind that young children tire easily, so keep the party short and the food simple.

THREE TO FIVE

Children in this age group are old enough to enjoy parties thoroughly. They make friends easily and play happily together with children of the same age.

Food should have visual appeal, but be kept as simple as possible. Jelly and ice cream are old favourites with this age group. It's best to have the party out of doors where it doesn't matter if they make a mess and they can all run around to their heart's content when they've finished eating.

Keep games short and simple and provide crayons and drawing paper to keep them occupied. On a cold or rainy day it would be a good idea to rent a Walt Disney video to show after everyone's had enough to eat.

SIX TO NINE

At this age, a party is a significant event in any child's life. The birthday cake is of paramount importance and should fire the child's imagination. A maximum of 10 children should be invited, as they are very energetic and lively at this age and could easily get out of hand. Mums should not be invited as they could inhibit the spontaneous atmosphere – besides you will have enough to do without having to worry about entertaining the mums.

Plan the party around a theme and ask the children to dress accordingly. Play team games or organise entertainment suitable to the theme.

Provide savoury and sweet food in equal quantities and remember the classics – crisps, marshmallows and ice cream.

At certain ages it is better to have single-sex parties. Boys and girls from around seven to nine are inclined to regard the other sex as a nuisance; the boys are normally very energetic and rough while the girls tend to be more sedate.

But always leave it up to the birthday child to decide who gets invited. And if the list happens to include both boys and girls, just ensure that the playing does not turn into fighting.

PARTIES FOR PRE-TEENS

Youngsters from 10 to 12 love being treated like adults, so preparing a party for this age group should be similar to preparing one for adults. At this age they often want more substantial snacks than the sweets and cakes served at parties for younger children.

The menu should be simple and informal – variety is not as important as quantity as we all know how much young boys can consume – and let them help themselves. The best would be to choose a central theme and plan everything accordingly.

There can never be enough potato crisps, peanuts, popcorn, raisins or fruit at these parties. If your youngster does not fancy the idea of a heavily decorated birthday cake, a tart or simple carrot or orange cake can be served for dessert.

Youngsters love being involved in the preparation of the food; a hamburger, fondue, braai or pancake party, will therefore be most suitable.

Children from this age group prefer parties in the evening, but it is important that they know when it will end – the duration depends on the age of the youngsters – and you will have to make certain that everyone has a lift home.

Drinks will depend on the age group. Homemade ginger beer or fruit punch is popular but see that there are enough chilled cool drinks – especially if there is going to be dancing!

Appearances can be deceiving – these youngsters can be very shy, especially in mixed company. Suggest a few games, but allow them to decide which ones they would like to play; these youngsters have their own ideas about games and fun. Good icebreakers are pairing games such as 'Find your Mate', 'Elly Rose', 'Twos and Threes', or 'Adam and Eve'.

It's important to play the right music, even if it does just sound like a lot of noise! A good idea is to ask each guest to bring along his or her favourite CD – that way you won't have to worry about the music not being suitable. But think of the neighbours and keep the decibels down!

Last but not least, parents shouldn't be visible but should keep an unobtrusive eye on the proceedings.

CARDS

Although a wide variety of printed invitations is available from shops these days, it is far more rewarding to design and make your own unique invitations, not to mention cheaper. The end result is also much more personal.

Design the invitations according to the theme chosen for the party or use a general design suitable for any theme. All the invitations included in the themes are very easy to make and will take you no more than a few minutes each. Be creative and design your own invitations – have your children help and give ideas too.

It's also a good idea to make place cards that match the invitations and theme. An alternative to making place cards is to write each friend's name on his or her own box or bag. Fill the boxes or bags with sweets to take home.

BOXES AND BAGS

Serving the snacks in boxes or bags is a far easier alternative to giving each child a plate. Then the children can eat when and as much as they want.

What ever is left over towards the end of the party, can be taken home in the box or bag. It surely makes the clean-up process easier and you won't have half eaten sweets lying around.

The basic boxes and bags illustrated here can be adapted to suit nearly any theme.

SCORE

Use a blunt object, such as a knitting needle or empty ball-point pen, and pull it across the cardboard to leave a distinct mark. Be sure not to cut the paper. This technique is used where the cardboard has to be folded.

ANIMAL FACE BOXES
coloured corrugated cardboard
steel ruler and pencil
scissors
glue

Draw the design of the box onto the back of the cardboard according to the diagram on page 95. Cut out along the solid lines and score along the dotted lines.

Carefully fold along the scored lines. Fold the tabs to the inside and glue them to the sides. Fold the rounded tabs of the lid to the inside and close the lid.

Decorate the box with an animal face cut from cardboard as shown.

STAR BOX

This beautiful star box will catch any child's favour. Fill them with sweets or little presents to take home. These easy to follow steps will help you make them in no time.

cardboard in an interesting
texture or pretty colour
steel ruler and pencil
scissors, craft knife and cutting mat
glue

Trace the pattern of the star onto the back of the textured cardboard according to the diagram on page 94. Cut out the pattern along the solid lines and score along the dotted lines.

Perforate the lines marked with dots by cutting through the cardboard along these lines at short intervals (use the sharp end of the craft knife). Carefully fold the card-board along the scored and perforated lines to complete the star shape.

Fold the sides at A to F at the bottom pentagon and glue to the sections of the top pentagon with corresponding letters. It should look like diagram 2 on page 94.

Fold along the scored and perforated lines again to achieve depth. Insert the snacks into the box through the unglued flap.

PIRATE'S BAG

black cardboard
scissors
glue
steel ruler and pencil
material for decorating
punch
white string or cord

Draw the pattern onto the back of the cardboard according to the diagram on page 96. Cut out along the solid lines and score along the dotted lines. Carefully fold the cardboard along the scored lines. Fold over the edge and glue together firmly.

Use a punch and pierce holes on both sides to thread cord for the handles. Glue the sides of the bag first, then the bottom.

Thread cord or string through the holes for the handles and make a knot to keep it in position.

Decorate the bag with a picture of skull and cross bones.

Adapt the colour and decorations on the bag to suit your theme.

MILK BOTTLE BASKET

empty 2-litre plastic milk bottle
sharp knife
material to decorate

Wash the milk bottles and allow to dry. Cut out a basket as shown on the photograph. Decorate with florists' ribbon and plastic insects or according to your theme.

CANDY BAGS

gingham material
sweets
ribbon
candy cane

Use cheap colourful fabric, preferably gingham, or any pieces of left over fabric you might have lying around. Cut out a 30 cm square for each child attending the party. Place sweets in the middle and pull the corners together. Tie it with colourful ribbon and for a finishing touch place a candy cane through the ribbon.

Creepy-crawly!

This is an ideal theme for toddlers who are fascinated by the insect world. Give your imagination free rein and let them experience creepy-crawlies in a positive way!

MENU

Beautiful butterfly cake
Lovely ladybirds
Chocolate beetles
Super spiders
Savoury bread snacks
Wobbly Willy Worm
Bee nectar

GAMES & ENTERTAINMENT

Making party bee boxes
Crawling ants
Insect antics
Blowing bubbles
Funny faces

DECORATIONS

- Make feelers out of pipe cleaners or stiff paper for each child to wear as a crown.
- Make place cards in the shape of different insects and draw colourful worms or bees on each paper plate.
- Cut green serviettes in the shape of leaves.
- Colour marshmallow paste* and make bees, beetles or worms with liquorice feelers.
- Make little baskets out of milk bottles for the toddlers to take their sweets home in (see page 15).

INVITATIONS

This is an easy invitation that the birthday girl or boy will love to help make. Cut folded paper into the shape of a butterfly, ensuring that the fold runs through the middle of the butterfly's body (see diagram). Paint the wings in bright colours and print the details of the invitation on the inside of the card.

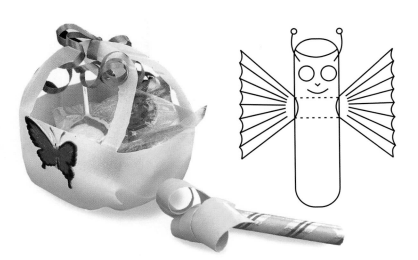

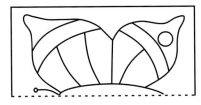

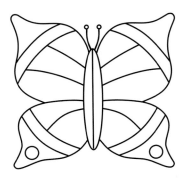

BIRTHDAY CAKE

BEAUTIFUL BUTTERFLY

1 x recipe for quick cake mix*
(size 2)
25 cm round cake tin
2 x recipe for butter icing*
40 g cocoa
brown food colouring
variety of sweets to decorate

Prepare and bake the cake (see recipe on page 89). When cool, cut and assemble the cake as shown in the illustration.

Mix the cocoa and butter icing to make chocolate icing – use brown food colouring to make it darker – and ice the cake. Decorate the butterfly with sweets as shown or to your liking.

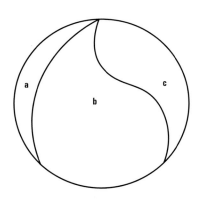

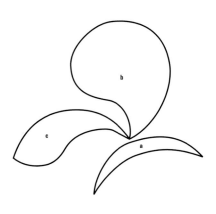

TIPS FOR DECORATING

If you struggle to get the icing dark enough, dissolve a little coffee powder with a few drops of water and mix it with the butter icing.

You can sprinkle coconut over the whole cake before decorating it with sweets.

Don't be shy to use a number of different colours and shapes of sweets. The brighter the butterfly, the more the children will love it.

SOMETHING SWEET

LOVELY LADYBIRDS

1 x recipe for quick cake mix*
(size 1)
1 x recipe for butter icing*
red food colouring
shoestring liquorice
Smarties
silver balls

Prepare and bake 24 cup-cakes (see recipe on page 89). Colour the butter icing bright red and ice each cupcake.

Decorate with liquorice, Smarties and silver balls to resemble ladybirds. If you prefer to avoid food colouring, use chocolate icing instead (mix cocoa with butter icing).

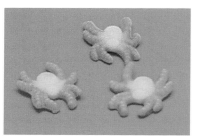

CHOCOLATE BEETLES

1 packet Marie biscuits
250 ml condensed milk
30 ml cocoa
dark chocolate vermicelli
shoestring liquorice
silver balls

Break the Marie biscuits into pieces and crush finely. Add the condensed milk and cocoa and mix very well. Shape into balls and roll in the vermicelli. Cut liquorice into small pieces for the legs and press in silver balls for eyes.

SAVOURY TREATS

SUPER SPIDERS

small, round bread rolls
butter or margarine
cheese, grated
Niknaks
raisins or cocktail onions
lettuce leaves

Slice each bread roll in half, closer to the top. Spread with butter or margarine, and put some grated cheese in the middle. Press Niknaks into the roll to resemble legs and use raisins or cocktail onions for the eyes. Arrange the super spiders on lettuce leaves.

SAVOURY BREAD SNACKS

white bread
butter or margarine
Marmite
finely grated biltong or crushed
potato crisps

Slice the bread into 3 cm thick slices, remove the crusts and cut each slice into 6 cubes. Mix butter or margarine with Marmite and cover each cube thoroughly. Roll the cubes in grated biltong or crushed potato crisps.

DESSERT

WOBBLY WILLIE WORM

2 packs green jelly powder
vanilla ice cream
2 red glacé cherries
liquorice

Make jelly according to the instructions on the packet and refrigerate until set. Cut jelly into small cubes and place on a flat tray or in a shallow bowl.

Scoop a ball of ice cream for each child onto the jelly to resemble a worm. Add cherries for the eyes and liquorice for feelers and serve immediately.

DRINKS

BEE NECTAR

1 x 410 g can pear halves
1 x 410 g can peach slices
1 x 425 g can crushed
pineapple
1 x 113 g can granadilla pulp
500 ml orange juice
500 ml apple juice
a handful of glacé cherries
1 litre chilled lemonade
1 litre chilled soda water

Blend pears, peaches and pineapple with the juice. Add granadilla pulp, orange juice, apple juice and cherries and chill in the refrigerator. Add lemonade and soda water before serving. Makes 20 glasses.

Pirates of Penzance

Any child between the ages of five and nine would love an invitation to a pirate party. It is most suitable for little boys who love to fight off the enemy and search for hidden treasure. Give each little pirate his or her own eye patch – made from black cardboard or stiffened fabric with thin elastic to fit around the head – as they arrive. Make bandannas from scraps of fabric to further add to the theme of the party.

MENU

Treasure chest cake
Pirate faces
Jewellery cases
Bread wheels
Pirate ships
Nuggets
Cannonballs
Buccaneer strawberry foam
Captain Hook's punch

GAMES & ENTERTAINMENT

Grab-a-treasure
Treasure hunt 1
Treasure hunt 2
Highwayman
Cops and Robbers

INVITATIONS

sheets of onion skin writing paper
kebab sticks
glue
raffia or red florist's ribbon

Singe the edges of the paper before printing the details. Ask each child to come dressed as a pirate and to bring along pirate paraphernalia such as a telescope or plastic sword. Glue a kebab stick to each side of the paper and roll towards the centre like a parchment scroll. Tie the scroll with a small piece of raffia or red florists' ribbon.

DECORATIONS

- Try making all decorations in red, black and white if possible. Use red and white serviettes and provide a red balloon for each child to take home.
- Make paper flags and draw sculls and crossbones on them. Smaller flags can be placed in each plate or bowl of eats.
- Make a different place card that fits the theme for every guest.
- To further enhance the theme, use plastic daggers, beads and earrings, an anchor and a big map charting the position of the hidden treasure.
- Plastic crabs, shells, a bunch of keys and a couple of spades can also be used as props.
- Have watercolours on hand for those who forgot their tattoos and wounds.

BIRTHDAY CAKE

TREASURE CHEST

2 x recipe for quick cake mix*
(size 2)
2 rectangular cake tins
2 x recipe for butter icing*
25 ml cocoa
brown food colouring
chocolate coins, old bracelets, or
candy necklaces
Smarties and brightly wrapped
sweets
chocolate vermicelli
silver balls

Prepare and bake the cakes (see recipe on page 89). Allow to cool before cutting one cake in half, lengthwise. Use one half as the lid of the chest (see diagram).

Mix butter icing with cocoa and brown food colouring, keeping a small amount of butter icing for the line decorations (see photo). Use the icing to sandwich the remaining pieces together.

Ice the outside of the chest and lid and decorate further as shown, using chocolate coins, wrapped sweets and cheap jewellery for treasure.

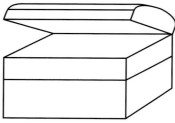

TIPS FOR DECORATING

- First cover the two sandwiched pieces of cake with icing and arrange the jewellery on top. Then ice the lid and position it as shown.
- If the lid needs propping up, use half a Flake on either side to keep it in place.

SOMETHING SWEET

PIRATE FACES

1 x recipe for quick cake mix
(size 1)
butter icing*
liquorice
multicoloured decorating balls

Prepare and bake 24 cup-cakes (see recipe on page 89). Ice each cup-cake and decorate with liquorice to resemble pirate faces.

JEWELLERY CASES

1 x recipe for pastry cases*
icing sugar
apricot, strawberry or blackberry
jam
prepared custard

Prepare and bake the pastry cases (see recipe on page 89). When cool, sift icing sugar over. Spoon jam and custard into each pastry case and serve.

SAVOURY TREATS

BREAD WHEELS
white bread
butter or margarine
vienna sausages

Slice the bread thinly and remove the crusts. Butter slices lightly, place a Vienna sausage on each slice of bread and roll up. Slice across to form wheels, securing with cocktail sticks, if necessary.

CANNONBALLS
450 – 500 g minced beef
1 onion, finely chopped
50 g fresh breadcrumbs
1 egg
salt and pepper

Preheat oven to 160°C. Mix all the ingredients together thoroughly. Form mixture into balls the size of walnuts and place on a greased baking tray. Bake for about 20 minutes or until brown and crisp. Serve on lettuce leaves or in small paper cases.

Makes about 30 cannonballs.

PIRATE SHIPS
cheese scones
cheese squares
cocktail sticks
red cocktail onions
butter or margarine

Cut each scone in half and spread with butter or margarine. Cut the cheese square diagonally to form the sails.

Thread the cocktail stick through the cheese to form a sail, and stick it into the scone. Place a small piece of red cocktail onion onto the end of the cocktail stick.

You can add a small flag with the skull and crossbones to further decorate the ships.

NUGGETS
240 g whole-wheat flour
20 ml baking powder
pinch of salt
200 g cheese, grated
450 ml milk

Preheat oven to 220°C. Sift the dry ingredients together and add the cheese. Make a well in the dry ingredients and stir in the milk to form a soft dough.

Drop spoonfuls of the mixture onto a greased baking sheet. Bake for 15 minutes.

Makes 50 nuggets.

DESSERT

BUCCANEER STRAWBERRY FOAM
1 packet strawberry jelly powder
125 ml evaporated milk, chilled
125 g strawberries, pureed

Make the jelly according to the instructions on the packet, leave until cool but not set. Add the chilled evaporated milk and beat until the mixture is stiff. Fold in the strawberries and pour into moulds. Place in the refrigerator to set.

DRINKS

CAPTAIN HOOK'S PUNCH
1 litre Coca-Cola
1 litre lemonade
1 litre water
1 litre soda water
350 ml granadilla squash
350 ml orange squash
1 x 410 g can mixed fruit
2 bananas, sliced

Chill all the ingredients, except the fruit, in refrigerator until ice cold and then mix together just before serving.

Makes 20 glasses.

Fairyland fantasy

Every little girl's favourite fantasy! Use a pink and white colour scheme for the decorations and food and ask each child to dress accordingly. Give the birthday girl a glittering crown and let her be a fairy princess on this special day.

MENU

Fairyland castle cake
Magical marsmallows
Rice Krispie fairy food
Watermelon balls
Dainty pink pastries
Polony kebabs
Dream dessert
Dreamy pink milkshakes

DECORATIONS

- Stars can be used in all of the decorations.
- Use pink, white and silver balloons, serviettes and confetti.
- The snacks themselves can serve as decorations, especially if they are mainly pink and white.
- Cut out pink and white cardboard stars to use as place cards.
- Make wands by covering sticks with foil and tying trailing strips of white, pink and silver crepe paper or tinsel to one end.
- Dainty flower arrangements on the table would look very pretty.

GAMES & ENTERTAINMENT

Find the sweets
Pass the present
Hire a magician
Rent a fairy-tale video

INVITATIONS

pink and white cardboard
glitter
glue
kebab sticks

Cut stars out of the cardboard and decorate with glitter. Print the details on the other side, and glue a kebab stick to the star.

BIRTHDAY CAKE

FAIRYLAND CASTLE

1 x recipe for quick cake mix*
(size 2)
square cake tin
2 x recipe for butter icing*
red food colouring
4 pink ice cream cones
sweets and silver balls to
decorate

Prepare and bake the cake (see recipe on page 89). When cool, cut the cake according to the diagram and assemble as shown. Colour the butter icing pale pink and ice the cake.

Position the ice cream cones for the towers and decorate to resemble a castle. Fill the 'courtyard' with marshmallows or other pink and white sweets.

TIPS FOR DECORATING

- The icing shouldn't be too bright, it must be kept fairy-like.
- The sweets that you use to decorate the cake should be either silver or pastel coloured.
- If you don't have time to make marshmallows, bought ones are a suitable alternative.
- Small fairy dolls can be placed around the cake and given as prizes at the end of the party.

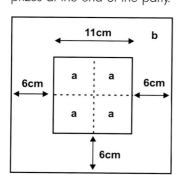

SOMETHING SWEET

MAGICAL MARSHMALLOWS

15 ml gelatine
60 ml cold water
60 ml boiling water
210 g castor sugar
5 ml vanilla essence
red food colouring
icing sugar for rolling

Spray a 2,5 litre casserole with non-stick baking spray. Soak the gelatine in the cold water until spongy. Place over simmering water and heat slowly until gelatine has dissolved.

Add boiling water and castor sugar and beat for 7-10 minutes with an electric beater until mixture begins to thicken. Add vanilla and a few drops of red food colouring and mix well. Pour into the prepared casserole.

Chill in the refrigerator until set, then cut into squares and roll in icing sugar.

Makes about 30 marshmallows.

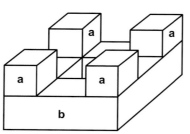

RICE KRISPIE FAIRY FOOD

100 g butter or margarine
100 g pink marshmallows
100 g caramelised condensed milk
100 g pink Rice Krispies

Heat butter or margarine, marshmallows and condensed milk over low heat until all ingredients have melted. Remove from stove and add Rice Krispies. Mix well.

Press firmly into a well-greased Swiss roll tin. Cut into squares while still slightly warm. Remove when completely cool.

Makes about 60 squares.

WATERMELON BALLS

Prepare a large bowl of watermelon balls for a summer party. If refrigerated before the party, it makes for a welcoming cool snack. Watermelon is a favourite amongst most children and is far healthier than sweets.

SAVOURY TREATS

DAINTY PINK PASTRIES
1 x recipe for pastry cases*
30 ml butter or margarine
30 ml cake flour
pinch of salt
200 ml milk
3 Vienna sausages, chopped
50 ml grated cheese

Prepare and bake the pastry cases (see recipe on page 89). For the filling, melt the butter or margarine, add flour and salt and stir until smooth.

Add the milk gradually, stirring over medium heat until sauce is thick and smooth. Add Vienna sausages and cheese, mix well and leave to cool. Fill pastry cases with mixture just before serving.

Fills about 30 cases.

POLONY KEBABS
4 small polonies
cheddar cheese
cocktail sticks

Cut the polony in 5 mm thick slices and quarter each slice. Cut 5 mm thick slices of cheese into cubes of about 1 cm x 1 cm.

String polony triangles and cheese cubes onto cocktail sticks to make kebabs.

DESSERT

DESSERT DREAM
1 packet red jelly powder
250 ml boiling water
375 ml evaporated milk, well chilled
50 ml sugar
whipped cream
glacé cherries

Dissolve jelly powder in boiling water and leave to cool. Beat evaporated milk and sugar together until thick. Add jelly and mix well.

Spray a jelly mould with non-stick baking spray, pour in jelly mixture and place in refrigerator until set. Turn out onto a plate and decorate with whipped cream and glacé cherries.

Enough for 8–10 portions.

DRINKS

DREAMY PINK MILKSHAKES
3 litres milk
1 litre strawberry ice cream

Blend milk and ice cream together until frothy. Serve in plastic or cardboard cups.

Makes 25–30 small glasses.

Forest fun

This theme is based on the story of Hansel and Gretel. Place the table with the birthday cake in such a way that the children have to trace it – this will set the mood right from the start. Wait until all the children have arrived, and then, using buttons or pieces of string as a guide, let them find the birthday cake. This theme has no set colour scheme – the brighter the better.

MENU

Log cabin cake
Nutty logs
House biscuits
Bread pancakes
Cheese balls
Mountain dew
Banana lollipops

GAMES & ENTERTAINMENT

Find the sweets
Follow-my-leader
Hot potato
Find your partner
Highwayman

INVITATIONS

brightly coloured paper

Use white paper, cut into the shape of a house, for the base of your card. Cut yellow paper for the wall and red for the roof of the house. Cut a door and two windows in the yellow paper, before pasting it onto the base. Write the details of the invitation in the door and windows (see photo).

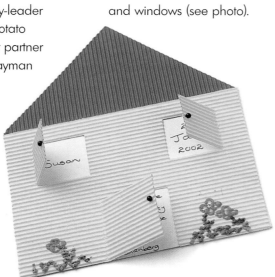

DECORATIONS

- Most of the decorations will be on the table. Use brightly coloured serviettes and name cards in the shape of logs.
- Brightly coloured balloons will help create a festive atmosphere.
- Hang streamers, strips of green crepe paper and tinsel from the ceiling to the door knobs to create a forest atmosphere.
- Make toadstools from marshmallow paste* and candy trees to place on the table. Make a traveling bag for each child (see instructions on page 15) and fill with sweets to take home.

BIRTHDAY CAKE

LOG CABIN

2 x recipe for quick cake
mix* (size 2)
3 bread tins
2 x recipe for butter icing*
variety of sweets
Chomps for the roof
desiccated coconut
green food colouring
2 chocolate Flakes

Prepare and bake the cakes (see recipe on page 89). When cool, cut and assemble the cake as shown in the illustration.

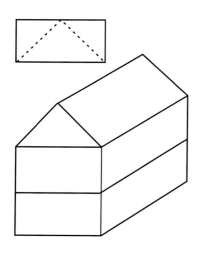

Place cake on a square cake board covered with foil. Cover the cake with butter icing, and decorate with sweets as shown.

Colour the desiccated coconut with green food colouring and sprinkle around the cake. Break the Flakes to resemble logs.

TIPS FOR DECORATING

- To make the roof, use either plain, flat chocolate squares, or to create a thatched roof, marshmallows covered in toasted coconut.
- Ice the entire cake with light brown icing and draw slightly uneven lines on the icing with a cocktail stick to resemble a real log cabin, or cover with Flakes.

SOMETHING SWEET

NUTTY LOGS

50 ml oil
40 ml honey
20 ml soft brown sugar
150 g oats
60 ml seedless raisins
60 ml chopped nuts
200 g milk chocolate, melted

Preheat oven to 180°C. Mix oil and honey, add sugar and mix well. Add oats, raisins and nuts and mix.

Press mixture into a greased Swiss roll tin or baking tray.

Bake for 30 minutes, leave to cool slightly and then cut into bars.

Dip bars in melted chocolate and draw stripes on them to resemble logs as soon as the chocolate has set. Makes 24 logs.

HOUSE BISCUITS

Marie biscuits
Italian wafer biscuits in different colours
royal icing*
variety of sweets

Cut Italian wafer biscuits in half and cut one half into triangles to make the roofs for the houses.

Attach the wafer squares and triangles to the Marie biscuits with royal icing.

Decorate with sweets to resemble houses.

SAVOURY TREATS

BREAD PANCAKES

white bread
butter or margarine
cheese spread
finely grated biltong or crushed potato crisps
cocktail sticks

Slice bread thinly and remove crusts. Flatten slices with a rolling pin and spread each slice with butter or margarine and cheese spread.

Sprinkle with finely grated biltong or crushed crisps. Roll up like a pancake and secure with a cocktail stick if necessary.

CHEESE BALLS

250 g mashed potato
250 g grated cheddar cheese
1 egg
60 g cake flour
3 ml baking powder
pinch each of salt, pepper and
paprika
dried breadcrumbs
oil for deep-frying

Mix all the ingredients together, pinch off pieces and roll into balls.

Deep-fry in hot oil until golden brown.

Drain on absorbent kitchen paper and serve on cocktail sticks.

Makes about 60 cheese balls.

DRINKS

MOUNTAIN DEW

Serve a variety of chilled fruit juices in different colours in brightly coloured cups. Grape, orange and pineapple juice not only tastes good, but is also healthy and looks festive.

DESSERT

BANANA LOLLIPOPS

6 ripe, but firm bananas
lemon juice
12 kebab sticks
250 g dark baking chocolate
chopped nuts

Peel bananas and cut in half. Dip the bananas in lemon juice to prevent them discolouring.

Insert a kebab stick in each half. Dip bananas in melted chocolate and allow to set slightly before rolling in chopped nuts.

Cover the bananas in foil as soon as the chocolate has set and refrigerate until required.

Makes 12 lollipops.

We have lift-off!

Every child dreams of becoming an astronaut at some stage in his or her life. This theme will give youngsters a chance of taking a dream trip to the moon where they can meet all kinds of weird and wonderful beings from outer space.

MENU

Spaceship cake
Spacecraft
Martians
Flying saucers
Space kebabs
Orbital ice cream
Moon juice

GAMES & ENTERTAINMENT

Unroll the toilet paper
Eating chocolate
Grab-a-treasure
Rent a science fiction video

INVITATIONS

MOON AND STARS INVITATION
stiff paper, folded in half
silver paper or paper covered
with foil
green felt-tipped pen

Cut silver paper in the shape of moons and stars and glue onto each card. Write the details on the inside with a thick green felt-tipped pen.

DECORATIONS

- With the birthday cake being a spaceship, the decorations should follow the space theme - shiny stars, planets and rockets.
- Hang silver tinsel, stars and moons from the ceiling.
- Make moon and star place cards.
- Make a rocket container for the children to take their sweets home in (see instructions that follow).

ROCKET CONTAINERS
empty toilet paper rolls
glue
paper or cardboard
small sweets and toys
foil

Paste paper or cardboard over one open end of each roll. Make the pointed nose of the space rocket by cutting paper or cardboard circles from the edge to the center. Overlap the cut edges and glue them in position to form funnels.

Fill each container with sweets and a toy. Cover the toilet rolls and the rockets' noses with foil, then glue a nose onto each roll.

Cover triangular pieces of cardboard with foil to resemble fins, and glue to the sides of each space rocket. Stick red dots onto each rocket for lights and place cotton wool between the fins to resemble smoke.

If you don't have enough toilet paper rolls, cut the cardboard holder for aluminium foil in three.

BIRTHDAY CAKE

SPACE SHIP
2 Swiss rolls
kebab stick
firm cardboard
foil or silver paper
2 x recipe for royal icing*
sweets to decorate
silver balls
candy floss (optional)

Cut one Swiss roll in half. Place one half on top of the whole Swiss roll to make the spaceship. Use a kebab stick to secure the cakes if they aren't stable. Cover the cake with royal icing and decorate with sweets as shown in the photograph.

Cut the cardboard into 3 or 4 triangles, and cover them neatly with foil or shiny wrapping paper to resemble fins. Position the fins around the spaceship. Make a cone out of cardboard for the nose of the spaceship. Position the nose on the cake and decorate with butter icing.

Make moon rocks according to the recipe for popcorn-lollies on page 43 – omit jelly powder and food colouring – and place them around the spaceship.

TIPS FOR DECORATING

- Try to make all the snacks and sweets in more or less the same colours. This theme should not be multi-coloured.
- Dip your knife or spatula into hot water when finishing the icing, this will ensure a streamlined spaceship.
- Silver balls are ideal for decorating this cake.
- Serve the remaining half of the Swiss roll in slices.

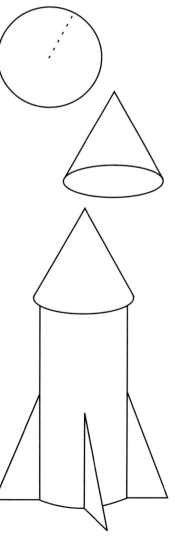

SOMETHING SWEET

SPACECRAFT
ice cream cones
sweets
royal icing*
Marie biscuits
Italian wafer biscuits
silver balls
red Smarties

Fill ice cream cones with sweets and stick a Marie biscuit to each cone using royal icing.

Cut each Italian wafer biscuit diagonally to form 4 large triangles and stick the triangles to each ice cream cone to resemble the spacecraft's wings.

Decorate with silver balls and red Smarties.

MARTIANS
marshmallows
green royal icing*
Marie biscuits (optional)
shoestring liquorice
silver balls

Cover marshamallows with royal icing and stick one onto each Marie biscuit.

Decorate as shown in the photograph, using liquorice for the antennae and silver balls for the eyes.

DESSERT

ORBITAL ICE CREAM
1 packet raspberry jelly powder
vanilla ice cream
silver balls

Prepare the jelly according to the instructions on the packet and refrigerate until set. Chop the jelly coarsely and arrange in serving bowls. Place one or more scoops of ice cream in the center of each bowl and scatter with silver balls.

DRINKS

MOON JUICE
Serve fizzy cool drinks in colourful mugs. Call it 'Moon Juice' and see how much they enjoy it!

SAVOURY TREATS

FLYING SAUCERS
1 packet potato chips (cheese and onion)
5 slices white bread
1 packet Bacon Kips
Marmite
butter or margarine
10 small meat balls (see recipe for Canon balls page 23)
red and green cocktail onions
cocktail sticks

Crush the potato chips. Cut small circles, the size of the Bacon Kips, from the white bread with a cookie cutter or a small glass.

Mix a little Marmite with the butter or margarine and cover the bread circles completely. Roll in crushed potato chips and place on top of the Bacon Kips.

Cut the meat balls in half and put one half onto each bread circle. Secure the meat ball with a cocktail stick.

SPACE KEBABS
Vienna sausages
cheese
mushrooms
pineapple
cocktail tomatoes
cocktail sticks

Cut the sausages, cheese, mushrooms and pineapple into bite-size pieces. Combine all or a selection of these on cocktail sticks to make kebabs. A healthy, tasty snack!

Animal antics

There are an unlimited variety of cakes, sweets and savoury snacks that you could make in the shape of animals. We have given recipes for a few, but feel free to experiment and use your imagination to create your own collection of animal cookies and interesting snacks!

MENU

Prickly porcupine cake
Animal faces
Frog cups
Chocolate hedgehogs
Savoury swans
Cheese snakes
Ice cream mice
Apple and ginger fizz

ENTERTAINMENT

Crawling ants
Wolf, Wolf what's the time?
Insect antics
Crabs, crows and crayfish
Rent an animated Disney video
A visit to the zoo
Pony rides

INVITATIONS

cardboard
paint

Cut the cardboard into different animal shapes. Paint the animal onto the front of each card and print the details on the other side.

DECORATION

- Draw animal faces onto each child's paper plate.
- Make animal masks by painting faces on cardboard and cutting out the eyes and the mouths. Attach thin elastic to each mask to fit around a child's head.
- Make place cards in animal shapes.
- Make bunny boxes* and fill them with sweets for the children to take home. Party boxes decorated with animal faces will also work very well (see instructions on page 14).

BUNNY BOXES

paper or cardboard
glue
empty toilet paper roll
paint (non-toxic)
sweets
cotton wool

Paste a circle of paper or cardboard over one end of the toilet paper roll. Paint the rolls and leave to dry. Fill with sweets. Use cardboard to make the ears and cotton wool for the tail and glue into position.

BIRTHDAY CAKE

PRICKLY PORCUPINE

1 x recipe for quick cake mix
(size 2)
round cake tin (23cm)
white melting chocolate
chocolate covered pretzels
2 x recipe for butter icing*
50 g cocoa
sweets for the eyes

Prepare and bake the cake (see recipe on page 89). Cut and assemble the cake as illustrated.

Dip the ends of the pretzels into melted white chocolate. Leave to set. Mix the butter icing with the cocoa; use brown food colouring to make the icing darker.

Ice the cake and decorate with pretzels as shown. Use sweets for the eyes and nose.

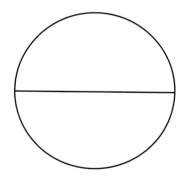

TIPS FOR DECORATING

- Use soft, brightly coloured sweets instead of the pretzels to make the porcupine quills.
- To prevent the pretzels from breaking when inserted into the cake, push holes into the cake with a kebab stick before inserting them.
- Flakes can also be used for quills. Refrigerate Flakes and carefully break them with the tip of a knife.
- Colour desiccated coconut green (see page 90), sprinkle onto a tray and position the porcupine on top.

SOMETHING SWEET

ANIMAL FACES

1 x recipe for quick cake mix*
(size 2)
colourful paper cases
2 x recipe for butter icing*
food colouring in different colours
sweets to decorate

Prepare and bake the cup-cakes, in paper cases (see recipe on page 89). Colour the butter icing different colours and decorate each cup-cake with icing and sweets to resemble animal faces.

FROG CUPS

royal icing*
wafer cups
Marie biscuits
sweets, nuts, raisins
butter icing*
food colouring

Use royal icing to attach two wafer cups together to form an open mouth as shown in the photograph. Stick each 'mouth' to a Marie biscuit with royal icing. Use sweets for eyes and attach with royal icing. Fill the 'mouth' with sweets, nuts and/or raisins.

Decorate the base with coloured butter icing.

CHOCOLATE HEDGEHOGS

225 g chocolate biscuits
150 g sugar
50 g cocoa
75 g softened butter or margarine
90 ml lukewarm milk
drinking chocolate powder
red glacé cherries, cut in half
blanched almonds, cut in strips

Crush the chocolate biscuits using a rolling pin. Mix with sugar and cocoa powder, gradually mix in the butter or margarine and milk.

Pinch off pieces or the mixture and shape into the form of hedgehogs. Roll in chocolate powder and use cherries for eyes and almond strips for the quills.

Makes about 20 hedgehogs.

SAVOURY TREATS

SAVOURY SWANS
hard-boiled eggs
mayonnaise
salt and pepper
lettuce leaves
potato crisps
cheese curls

Shell eggs and cut in half, length-wise. Remove yolks and mix to a soft paste with mayonnaise. Add salt and pepper to taste. Cut a small piece off the base of each egg so that it can stand. Carefully spoon the yolk mixture into the eggs and arrange on lettuce leaves. Use two potato crisps of the same size for each pair of wings and a cheese curl for the neck and head of the swan.

CHEESE SNAKES
250 g cake flour
2 ml salt
pinch of cayenne pepper
250 g butter or margarine
250 g grated Cheddar cheese
Marmite or Bovril

Preheat the oven to 200°C. Sift flour, salt and cayenne pepper together. Rub butter or margarine into the flour, add the cheese and mix well to form a firm, smooth dough. Pinch off pieces and roll into long, thin sausages. Paint patterns on the dough sausages with a small paintbrush and Marmite or Bovril, to resemble the markings on a snake.

Place on an ungreased baking tray and bake for about 6 minutes. Makes about 20–30 snakes.

DESSERT

ICE CREAM MICE
2 packets green and/or yellow jelly
chocolate, strawberry and/or vanilla ice cream
blanched almonds
shoestring liquorice
red glacé cherries

Prepare jelly according to the instructions on the packet and refrigerate until set. Chop the jelly and arrange in individual bowls. Place a scoop of ice cream into each bowl. Decorate with almonds for the ears, liquorice for the whiskers and tail, and cherries for the eyes and nose.

DRINKS

APPLE AND GINGER FIZZ
1 litre unsweetened apple juice
juice of 1 lemon
4 apples, peeled
1 litre ginger ale
ice cubes

Pour the apple and lemon juice into a large jug. Core and slice the apples and add to apple juice. Stir until the apple slices are covered, and chill. Add the ginger ale and ice cubes just before serving.
Makes 10 glasses.

Clown party

This theme is suitable for both boys and girls and can be extended to include the circus theme. Make or buy a clown hat for each guest, provide red noses and let them clown around to their hearts' content!

MENU

Rasta the clown cake
Popcorn-lollies
Clown surprises
Frankfurter twirls
Funny faces
Charlie the clown ice cream
Foolish floats

GAMES & ENTERTAINMENT

Follow-my-leader
Dressing up
Stop the music!
Insect antics
Visit the circus
Hire a magician

INVITATIONS

Make interesting pop-up invitations by following the instructions and illustrations given below.

A4 cardboard
glue
crayons or paint

Fold and cut paper in half. The one half is for the card and the other for the pop-up. Fold the piece for the pop up in half again. Cut out the shape of the clown, leaving a small space at the bottom of the paper for the tab. Open it out and colour it in. Fold the tabs back.

Measure the height of the clown from the top of the card and make a mark. Draw two lines diagonally from the mark to the bottom corners. Paste the clown on these lines, as shown in the diagram. Draw a picture on the front of the card and write all the details on the inside. Make sure that the pop-up doesn't protrude from the card when it is closed.

DECORATIONS

- This theme calls for a lot of colour so use a brightly coloured tablecloth, serviettes and balloons in assorted colours.
- Use brightly coloured cups and plates with a clown design.
- Let the children paint their faces with face paint and keep them busy with large balls and musical instruments.
- Make a clown container filled with sweets to give away as a prize to the best-dressed clown (see instructions on the following page).

CLOWN CONTAINER

2 litre plastic cool drink bottle
glue
scraps of wool
gummed paper
cardboard

Remove the label and cut the bottle just below the first curve. Glue wool scraps onto the container to resemble hair.

Cut out pieces of gummed paper to make a face and bow-tie and stick them onto the container as shown. Make a clown hat out of cardboard. Fill the bottle with sweets and then glue the hat onto the clown's head.

BIRTHDAY CAKE

RASTA THE CLOWN

2 x recipe for quick cake mix*
(size 2)
2 round cake tins (23 cm)
2 x recipe for butter icing*
Smarties
shoestring liquorice

Prepare and bake the cakes (see recipe on page 89). When cool, cut and assemble the cake as shown in the illustration.

Colour the butter icing and cover the cake, then decorate as shown in the photograph. Rasta's hair is made from shoestring liquorice.

TIPS FOR DECORATING

- Colour and decorate the cake as brightly as you wish. Use colourful sweets or add food colouring to the butter icing.
- As this cake is made up of many parts, it should be iced carefully so that the joints aren't visible.
- Flat pieces of Flake can also be used to resemble a clown's unkempt hair.
- Use florists' ribbon to make bowties; stick them to the cups to add to the theme.

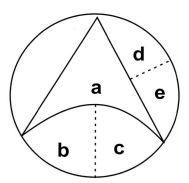

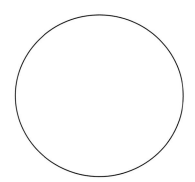

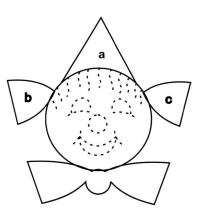

SOMETHING SWEET

POPCORN-LOLLIES

250 g unpopped popcorn
50 ml oil
500 g white marshmallows
1 packet green, red or yellow jelly powder
1 ml green, red or yellow food colouring
chopped nuts, glacé fruit and/or raisins (optional)
kebab sticks

Heat the oil in a large saucepan and pop the popcorn. Melt the marshmallows in another saucepan over very low heat, stirring continuously.

Add the jelly powder and food colouring to melted marshmallows. Stir in the popcorn and fruit and/or nuts and mix thoroughly.

Grease your hands with butter and shape mixture into balls. Press each ball firmly onto the end of a kebab stick and allow to cool.

Makes about 18 lollies.

CLOWN SURPRISE

ice cream cones
royal icing*
Marie biscuits
sweets
marshmallows
Smarties
butter icing*
silver balls

Cut off the conical-shaped portion of each cone and attach the ball to a Marie biscuit with royal icing. Fill the cone with sweets.

Attach a marshmallow (for the clown's head) with royal icing and then attach the sweet-filled cone (for his hat), as shown.

Decorate each clown's face and hat with Smarties, butter icing and silver balls.

SAVOURY TREATS

FRANKFURTER TWIRLS

Frankfurters
oil for deep-frying

Cut sausages into 3 cm pieces. Cut a cross, 1.5 cm deep, in one end of each piece.

Fry in hot oil until the ends of each sausage curl back and drain on absorbent kitchen paper.

FUNNY FACES

round bread rolls
butter or margarine
cocktail onions
Vienna sausages
grated cheese
small foil pie packs
lettuce leaves

Cut each bread roll in half and spread with butter or margarine. Arrange cocktail onions and sausages on each roll for eyes, mouth and nose and grated cheese for hair.

Arrange the 'faces' on lettuce leaves in the pie packs.

DESSERT

CHARLIE THE CLOWN ICE CREAM

ice cream
ice cream cones
Smarties
nuts
butter icing*

Place a scoop of ice cream in each bowl. Place a cone on top of each ball of ice cream for a hat and decorate with butter icing and Smarties. Serve immediately.

DRINKS

FOOLISH FLOATS

Serve an assortment of cool drinks in brightly coloured cups. Add a scoop of ice cream to each one and serve with straws decorated with florists' ribbon.

Ghost party

Most children, irrespective of their age, love listening to spooky stories. With this theme they have the opportunity of being ghosts themselves and enjoying a party at the same time.

MENU

Casper the Friendly Ghost cake
Halloween muffins
Meringue Ghosts
Eerie eggs
Ghoulish concoction
Ghosts' nests
Spooky floats

GAMES & ENTERTAINMENT

Highwayman
Ten little elves
Funny faces
And then...
Whispers
Rent a spooky video

INVITATIONS

Cut paper or cardboard in the shape of ghosts and write the details in lemon juice or vanishing ink. Add a rhyme in ordinary ink explaining how to read the message. Ask each child to come dressed as a ghost.

DECORATIONS

- Draw the curtains to create an eerie atmosphere and light a few candles (put well beyond the reach of little hands).
- Use a red, black and white colour scheme.
- Place a cracker next to each plate and make spooky masks out of paper plates.
- Cover the furniture with sheets.
- Draw or paint a skeleton onto an old sheet or large piece of paper and pin it to the curtains or over the windows.
- Hollow out large pumpkins, cut out the eyes and mouth and place a lighted candle in the hollow.
- Make small ghosts out of white marshmallow paste* with black sweets for eyes.

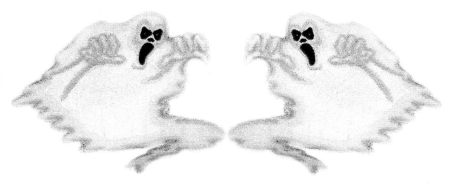

SOMETHING SWEET

HALLOWEEN MUFFINS
120 g cake flour
5 ml bicarbonate of soda
5 ml salt
400 g bran
250 ml milk
1 egg
125 ml honey

CREAM CHEESE ICING
30 ml butter or margarine
60 g smooth cottage cheese
60 g icing sugar
60 g castor sugar
5 ml vanilla essence
yellow and brown food colouring
(optional)
sweets to decorate

Preheat oven to 190°C. Sift the flour, bicarbonate of soda and salt into a mixing bowl. Stir in the bran. Whisk the milk and egg together and add the honey. Mix well.

Add the milk mixture to the dry ingredients and mix just until flour is moistened; batter should still be lumpy. Spoon into well-greased muffin tins and bake for 25 minutes. Remove carefully and allow to cool on wire rack.

Combine the butter or margarine, cottage cheese and icing sugar. Add castor sugar, beating until mixture is smooth. Add vanilla and colour icing two thirds yellow and the remainder brown.

Decorate the muffins, using the icing, to resemble Halloween masks.

Makes about 18 muffins.

BIRTHDAY CAKE

CASPER THE FRIENDLY GHOST
1 x recipe for quick cake mix*
(size 2)
1 rectangular cake tin
2 x recipe for royal icing*
sweets

Prepare and bake the cake (see recipe on page 89). Cut the cake according to the illustration.

Ice with royal icing and decorate with sweets as shown in the photograph.

TIPS FOR DECORATING
- Use a knife or fork to create an uneven texture.
- Preferably use only red and black sweets when decorating the cake.
- Arrange candy floss around the cake to make it look more eerie.
- Red-coloured coconut sprinkled around the cake creates a good contrast. The cake can also be placed on a black tray.

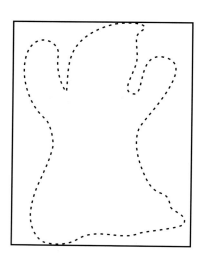

Meringue ghosts

meringue mix*
Marie biscuits
white royal icing*
shoestring liquorice

Preheat oven to 120°C. Prepare meringue mix according to the recipe on page 90. Spoon meringue in uneven heaps onto a greased baking sheet with two spoons. Bake for 1 hour, switch off oven and leave meringues for another hour to dry out.

Cover each Marie biscuit with royal icing and top with a meringue. Use liquorice to make toes and eyes for each 'ghost'.

SAVOURY TREATS

Eerie eggs

hard-boiled eggs
raisins
cheese spread
cheese, cut into strips

Shell eggs and stick two raisins on each egg with cheese spread, to resemble eyes. Make two small holes on either side of each egg and stick in cheese strips to resemble arms.

Ghoulish concoction

45 ml butter or margarine
45 ml cake flour
salt and pepper
250 ml milk
100 g shredded tuna
30 pastry cases*
Niknaks

Melt the butter or margarine and stir in the flour and seasoning. Gradually add the milk, stirring until sauce is thick and smooth. Bring to the boil, reduce heat and simmer for 2 minutes. Remove from heat and stir in tuna. Just before serving, spoon the mixture into pastry cases and place a Niknak in each to resemble a spoon.

Makes 30 cases.

DESSERT

Ghosts' nests

meringue mix*
vanilla ice cream
silver balls

Prepare meringue mix according to the recipe on page 90 and spread or pipe circles onto a greased baking sheet. Bake as instructed and allow to cool.

Place a scoop of ice cream on each meringue circle and sprinkle with silver balls.

DRINKS

Spooky floats

2 litre Coca-Cola
500 ml vanilla ice cream

Pour cool drink into glasses and spoon the ice cream on top.

Sufficient for 10–15 glasses.

What a pretty hat!

Girls aged six to eight love to dress up and play Madame – if there's a bag full of mom's old clothing and hats, the games can begin in earnest. With this theme little girls can pretend they're attending a proper grand tea party!

MENU

Hat cake
Little hats
Dainty Cupcakes
Necklaces and bracelets
Ginger hats
Pretty Pastries
Rainbow rolls
Banana snow surprise
Hot chocolate with marshmallows

GAMES & ENTERTAINMENT

Crawling ants
Fashion parade
Dressing-up
What's different
Ten little elves
Whispers

INVITATIONS

Make hat shaped invitations in different forms and colours. Ask each friend to wear a hat to the party. Give a prize at the party for the most original hat.

DECORATIONS

- The children themselves are the decorations in this theme.
- Hold a fashion parade to allow each friend to show off her hat.
- Provide extra hats for those who arrive without one.
- Use pretty serviettes and place cards to decorate the table. Provide balloons to take home.
- Place simple fresh flower arrangements on the table.

Lisa

BIRTHDAY CAKE

HAT CAKE

1 x recipe for quick cake mix*
(size 2)
1 x recipe for quick cake mix*
(size 1)
round cake tin (20cm)
round cake tin (25cm)
2 x recipe for butter icing*
yellow food colouring
sweets and marshmallows

Mix and bake the cakes (see recipe on page 89). Bake size 1 in the 20 cm cake tin, and size 2 in the 25 cm tin.

Place the smaller cake on top of the bigger one. If you want to create a bigger contrast the top cake can be cut smaller.

Colour the butter icing yellow and ice the cake as shown. Use the sweets to decorate to taste.

SOMETHING SWEET

LITTLE HATS

marshmallows
royal icing*
Marie biscuits
glacé icing
hundreds and thousands
silver balls

Secure each marshmallow to a Marie biscuit with royal icing. Cover with Glacé icing and decorate with Hundreds and thousands or silver balls.

GLACÉ ICING

sifted icing sugar
hot water
food colouring

Mix the icing sugar and hot water to a smooth coating consistency. Colour if desired.

DAINTY CUPCAKES

1 x recipe for quick cake mix*
(size 1)
1 x recipe for butter icing*
sweets to decorate
food colouring

Mix and bake the cupcakes (see instructions on page 89). Decorate with butter icing and sweets as shown or to taste.

NECKLACES AND BRACELETS

Thread any soft sweets, such as Jelly Tots or Liquorice Allsorts, onto thread or hat elastic to make necklaces and bracelets. If you're pressed for time, you can buy ready made sweet necklaces from sweet shops.

GINGER HATS

225 g cake flour
10 ml ground ginger
pinch of salt
115 g margarine
180 g soft brown sugar
1 egg, beaten

GLAZE

1 egg yolk
25 ml milk

Preheat oven to 190°C. Sift the cake flour, ginger and salt. Rub the margarine into the dry ingredients until the mixture resembles fine breadcrumbs. Add the sugar and mix in. Add the egg and mix until a dough forms. Place the dough in a plastic bag and cool in the refrigerator.

Flour a pastry board and roll the dough out thinly. Cut into hat shapes and arrange on a greased baking sheet.

Beat the egg yolk and milk and paint on the gingerbread. Bake for 8–10 minutes until golden brown. Makes 30 hats.

SAVOURY TREATS

RAINBOW ROLLS

1 loaf day-old white bread
80 g butter or margarine
60 g cheese spread
2 x 20cm long Vienna sausages
Marmite or Bovril

Cut the crusts off the bread and slice the loaf lengthwise into 8 thin slices measuring 20 cm x 8 cm. Mix half of the butter or margarine with cheese spread and the rest with Marmite or Bovril. Spread the cheese mixture on one slice bread, top with a second slice of bread and spread with the Marmite mixture. Place a third slice on top and spread with cheese mixture, and a fourth slice spread with Marmite mixture.

Place a Vienna sausage in the middle and roll the bread like a swiss roll. Wrap in waxpaper and refrigerate for a few hours.

Cut into 'wheels' and serve on lettuce leaves.

PRETTY PASTRIES

Make pastry cases (see recipe on page 89). Fill them with any of the following savoury fillings and garnish with chopped parsley.

- Make a white sauce and stir in grated Cheddar cheese.
- Mix liver sausage with cottage cheese and season with salt and pepper.
- Chop up Vienna sausages and stir into a thick white sauce.

DRINKS

HOT CHOCOLATE WITH MARSHMALLOWS

2 litres warm milk
120 ml hot chocolate
marshmallows

Mix well the ingredients with the warm milk. Beat until frothy. Pour into mugs and place two marshmallows in each drink.

DESSERT

BANANA SNOW SURPRISE

1 packed raspberry jelly powder
5 large, ripe bananas
15 ml lemon juice
1 egg white
30 ml sugar
10 red glacé cherries
hundreds and thousands

Prepare the jelly according to the instructions on the packet, pour into 10 individual bowls and refrigerate to set. Mash the bananas and add the lemon juice. Whisk the egg white until stiff, add to the banana mixture and beat until the mixture is creamy. Add sugar and beat until dissolved.

Spoon some of the mixture on top of the jelly in each bowl, place a glacé cherry in the centre and sprinkle with hundreds and thousands. Serves 10.

Abracadabra

There are so many variations on the theme of magic tricks and conjuring that you won't have to search far for ideas. From magical rabbits and brilliant white doves that are pulled from the magician's top hat, you also have wands, playing cards and a magnitude of other things that can be used with this theme. And just for fun make a candy Sangoma.

MENU

Top Hat cake
Toffee apples
Candy Sangomas
Playing cards
Gingerbread top hats
Cheesy magic wands
Bunny rolls
Banana split
Chocolate milkshake

INVITATIONS

cardboard
old playing cards

Fold cardboard in half and glue an old playing card onto the front. Write the details of the invitation inside the card.

DECORATIONS

- Make place cards from old playing cards.
- Use colourful serviettes, balloons and decorations.
- Make magic wands for each friend.

GAMES & ENTERTAINMENT

Dressing-up
Crabs, crows and crayfish
Eating chocolate
Rollerball
And then...
Hire a magician

BIRTHDAY CAKE

TOP HAT CAKE

1 x recipe for quick cake mix
(size 1)
1 x recipe for quick cake mix
(size 2)
square cake tin
rectangular cake tin
2 x recipe for Royal icing*
shoestring liquorice
sweets to decorate

Prepare and bake the cakes (see recipe on page 89). Use the square tin for size 1 and the rectangular tin for size 2. Cut and assemble as shown in the illustration. Ice and decorate as shown in the photograph, or to taste.

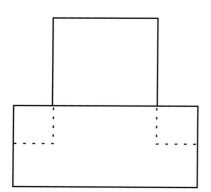

TIPS FOR DECORATING

- If you prefer to use butter icing. Instead of royal, use white margarine to ensure that the icing is snow-white.
- To make an interesting looking black Top Hat, buy black food colouring in powder form, available from a confectionery.

SOMETHING SWEET

TOFFEE APPLES

12 small red or green apples
12 kebab sticks
200 g sugar
40 ml water
40 ml golden syrup
10 ml margarine
5 ml vinegar
red, green or yellow food
colouring

Place well-greased waxed paper on a tray. Wash and dry the apples and push a kebab stick into each one.

Heat the sugar, water, golden syrup, margarine and vinegar over low heat and stir until the sugar has dissolved. Boil until the syrup forms hard brittle threads when dropped into cold water (hard ball stage). Add the colouring.

Dip each apple in the syrup, making sure that the whole apple is covered. Slowly remove from syrup and place on greased paper to cool and harden.

Makes 12 toffee apples.

CANDY SANGOMAS

any soft sweets
kebab sticks

Make candy Sangomas by threading sweets onto kebab sticks. See photograph.

PLAYING CARDS

Tennis biscuits
white royal icing*
black and red sweets – to cut
into shapes

Cover the Tennis biscuits with the royal icing. (You can use the left over royal icing from the Top Hat cake). Cut hearts, diamonds, clubs and spades from the red and black sweets and decorate the biscuits to resemble playing cards.

GINGERBREAD TOP HATS
100 g cake flour
3 ml bicarbonate of soda
3 ml ground ginger
60 g butter or margarine
80 ml soft brown sugar
30 ml honey
1 egg
silver balls

Preheat oven to 190°C. Sift the dry ingredients together and rub the butter or margarine into the dry ingredients until the mixture resembles fine breadcrumbs. Add the sugar and honey.

Beat the egg and add to the mixture to form a soft dough. Knead lightly and roll out on a floured surface to a thickness of approximately 6 mm.

Cut Top Hat shapes from the dough using a knife. Place the shapes on a greased baking sheet and decorate with silver balls. Bake for 12 minutes or until golden brown.

Makes 10–15 top hats.

SAVOURY TREATS

CHEESY MAGIC WANDS
175 g cake flour
pinch of salt
75 g butter
75 g cheese, grated
1 egg
2 egg yolks

Preheat oven to 180°C. Sift the flour and salt. Rub butter into the mixture. Add the cheese and bind the mixture with the egg to form a dough.

Roll out and cut into 1 cm x 20 cm long strips or roll into balls. Place strips on a baking sheet and brush with beaten egg yolks.

Bake for 10–15 minutes or until golden brown.

Makes about 24 wands.

BUNNY ROLLS
round rolls
butter or margarine
polony
cocktail sticks
cocktail onions
cheese
pretzels

Slice each roll in half horizontally. Butter each half and reassemble. Cut long ears out of polony and attach to each bread roll with cocktail sticks. Use onions, cheese and pretzels to make a face on each roll (see photo).

DESSERT

BANANA SPLITS
ice cream
bananas, sliced in half lengthwise
Italian wafer biscuits
hundreds and thousands

Place a scoop of ice cream in each bowl. Cut Italian wafer biscuits diagonally and arrange on the ice cream to resemble sails.

Place banana-halves on either side of the ice cream and decorate with hundreds and thousands.

DRINKS

CHOCOLATE MILKSHAKES
2 litres milk
500 ml chocolate ice cream
sprinkle nuts
chocolate vermicelli

Place milk and ice cream into a large bowl and beat with an electric beater. Pour into plastic glasses and decorate with nuts and vermicelli. Makes 10–15 glasses.

Come fly with me

This theme would be particularly suitable for boys between the ages of six and nine. At this age, they are fascinated by flying objects and often dream of becoming pilots. To keep the boys occupied, give them each a piece of paper, some string and bright ribbon and let them make their own kites that they can fly in the garden or nearby park. They can make paper jets and see whose jet can fly the furthest.

MENU

Colourful kite cake
Aeroplanes
Miniature kites
Clouds
Helicopters
Flight engineer kebabs
Squadron fruit kebabs
Pilots' fruit shake

INVITATIONS

cardboard
rope or string
paint
florists' ribbon
glue

Cut each piece of cardboard into the shape of a kite. Paint them in bright colours and make a tail out of florists' ribbon (see photo). Write the details of the party on the kite.

GAMES & ENTERTAINMENT

Treasure hunt 1
Cop and robbers
Follow-my-leader
Whispers
Take the children to a park where they can fly their kites

DECORATIONS

- Make small kites, aeroplanes and hot air balloons out of cardboard and hang them from the ceiling.
- Fold serviettes in the shape of a kite.
- Tie bows made from ribbon to the string attached to the balloons.
- Make a place card in the shape of a kite for each child.

BIRTHDAY CAKE

COLOURFUL KITE

2 x recipe for quick cake mix*
(size 1)
1 square cake tins
2 x recipe for butter icing*
shoestring liquorice
vermicelli (red and blue)
sweets to decorate
florists' ribbon for the tail

Prepare and bake the cake (see recipe on page 89). When cool, cut the cake according to the illustration. Ice the top and sides of the kite and decorate with liquorice and sweets as shown. Make a tail out of florists' ribbon (see photo).

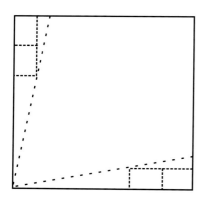

TIPS FOR DECORATING

- Make a bow to round off the tail of the kite.
- Place the kite cake on a blue background to resemble sky.
- Cut the left over pieces of cake into cubes, ice and use as an edible tail.

SOMETHING SWEET

AEROPLANES

Boudoir biscuits
Italian wafer biscuits
royal icing*
shoestring liquorice
sweets

Use a whole Boudoir biscuit and half a wafer for each aeroplane. Attach the wafer to the boudoir biscuit with royal icing to form the wings.

Cut a triangle from another wafer for the tail. Use short pieces of shoestring liquorice to resemble a propeller and decorate the aeroplane with sweets.

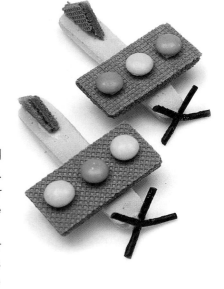

MINIATURE KITES

Italian wafer biscuits
shoestring liquorice
butter icing*
hundreds and thousands
variety of small, brightly coloured
sweets

Cut each wafer biscuit to resemble a kite. Use liquorice for the tail and decorate with butter icing, hundreds and thousands and sweets as shown.

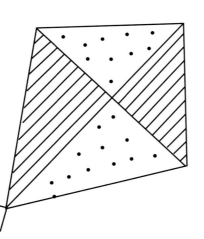

CLOUDS
158 g butter
250 ml castor sugar
22 ml vanilla essence
625 ml plain flour
1 egg

Preheat oven to 180°C. Mix butter, sugar and vanilla essence and beat until smooth. Add flour and egg and beat until a smooth dough forms. Knead dough lightly, wrap in plastic and refrigerate.

Flour a pastry board and roll the dough out thinly. Cut into cloud shapes and arrange on a greased baking sheet.

Bake for 10–12 minutes or until golden brown. Allow to cool. Decorate with royal icing to resemble clouds.

Makes about 30 cookies

SAVOURY TREATS

HELICOPTERS
Gouda cheese
large dill cucumbers
cocktail sticks

Cut the cheese into strips for the helicopter blades and attach to the dill cucumbers with cocktail sticks as shown.

FLIGHT ENGINEER KEBABS
Frankfurters, quartered
bacon rashers, halved and rolled up
cocktail tomatoes or tomato wedges
cocktail sticks
oil

Thread the ingredients alternately onto cocktail sticks.

Brush lightly with oil and grill in the oven for 5 minutes.

DESSERT

SQUADRON FRUIT KEBABS
bananas
lemon juice
seedless grapes
pineapple cubes
apricot halves
kebab sticks
ice cream

Slice bananas and sprinkle with lemon juice. Cube the other fruit and thread onto kebab sticks. Serve with ice cream.

DRINKS

PILOTS' FRUIT SHAKE
375 g soft fruit, such as bananas, peaches, strawberries or 225 g canned fruit
1,5 litres milk
1 litre vanilla ice cream
chocolate vermicelli

Wash and peel the fruit. Do not drain the fruit if using canned. Place the milk, ice cream, sugar and half the fruit in a blender and blend for approximately 45 seconds. If you are using canned fruit, add the juice as well.

Cut up the rest of the fruit and add to the milk mixture. Pour into glasses or mugs and decorate with chocolate vermicelli.

Makes 10–15 glasses.

The science fair

Erupting volcanoes, monstrous radioactive slimy worms, explosions and earthquakes will capture the imagination of any child. Combine this theme with science-related activities and games to make it even more fun and interesting.

MENU

Volcano cake
Mini volcanos
Radioactive worms
Volcanic rocks
Potato wedges
Sausage rolls
Ham and cheese rolls
Slimy punch
Ice cream with lava

INVITATION

Bright orange and brown
cardboard or paper
glue
scissors

Cut a volcano shape from the brown cardboard and paste it onto a white card. Decorate with paint and coloured cardboard to resemble a volcano erupting. Paste cotton wool to the top of the card to resemble smoke.

GAMES & ENTERTAINMENT

Unroll the toilet paper
Donkey
Rollerball
Make a Volcano

VOLCANO

1 x recipe for play dough*,
brown/green
15 ml baking soda
red food colouring
dishwashing liquid
62,5 ml vinegar

Set up a work area with newspaper, or use a surface that can get wet. This project can get messy.

Have the children model a volcano from brown or green play dough. You can use red clay around the rim of the volcano to make it look like flowing red-hot lava. Scoop out a hole at the top of the volcano and stir in the baking soda, a few drops of red food colouring, and a few drops of dishwashing liquid. When you're ready for the action, pour in the vinegar and stand back!

DECORATIONS

- Where possible use test-tubes and other laboratory goods to serve the food and drinks in. For example, test-tubes and cylinders for the drinks, and small glass bowls for the snacks.
- Fill glass jugs and bowls of differing sizes, with coloured water. Scatter the bowls around the room the party is being held in. When the friends start arriving, drop a piece of dried ice into each bowl. The water will bubble and smoke as a result. (Dried ice can be bought at most liquor stores.)
- Serve honeycomb in small bowls around the room, and invite the friends to eat some lava.

BIRTHDAY CAKE

VOLCANO CAKE

2 x recipe for quick cake mix*
(size 2)
ring tin
round cake tin (20cm)
60 g cocoa
3 slabs (250 g) dark chocolate
Crunchies
honeycomb

Add cocoa to the basic cake mix and bake cakes (see recipe on page 89). We use a ring tin as it already has the correct form. Cut the round cake according to the diagram.

Place pieces of Crunchie in the hollow. Melt the chocolate and pour it over the cake to resemble lava. Drop smaller pieces of honeycomb onto the cake to resemble lava rocks.

Store in a cool place to allow the chocolate to set.

MINI VOLCANOES

1 x recipe for quick cake mix
(size 1)
cocoa
Crunchies
1 slab dark chocolate

Add cocoa to the basic cake mix and bake 24 cup-cakes (see recipe on page 89). Break the Crunchies into small pieces and place on top of the cup-cakes.

Melt the dark chocolate and pour over the cupcakes to resemble mini volcanoes.

RADIOACTIVE WORMS

These worms are available from most sweet shops. Pour them into test-tubes and call them radioactive worms.

VOLCANIC ROCKS

1 can condensed milk
90 g butter or margarine
30 ml cocoa
200 ml chopped almonds
5 ml vanilla essence
250 ml crushed chocolate biscuits

Heat the condensed milk and butter or margarine over a low heat, in a saucepan. Add the cocoa and stir for 10 minutes. Remove from heat and add the almonds and vanilla.

Beat for 2 minutes. Add the chocolate biscuits and mix thoroughly. Scoop spoonfuls onto a greased baking sheet and refrigerate over night.

Makes 24 rocks.

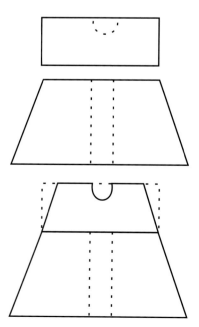

SAVOURY TREATS

POTATO WEDGES
8 large potatoes
oil
spices

Preheat oven to 200°C. Wash the potatoes and cut into wedges. Coat each piece with oil and sprinkle with chosen spices. Bake for 40 minutes until golden brown.

SAUSAGE ROLLS
12 slices white bread
30 ml mustard sauce
24 cocktail sausages
cocktail sticks
oil
tomato sauce

Preheat oven to 200°C. Remove the crusts and cut the bread in half diagonally. Spread lightly with mustard sauce. Roll each piece of bread around a sausage and secure with a cocktail stick. Lightly coat each roll with oil and bake for 5 minutes. Serve with tomato sauce.
Makes 24 rolls.

HAM AND CHEESE ROUNDS
240 g cake flour
20 ml baking powder
3 ml salt
25 ml butter or margarine
175 ml milk or milk and water
250 ml grated cheese
200 ml chopped ham

Preheat oven to 200°C. Sift the cake flour, baking powder and salt together. Rub margarine or butter into the dry ingredients. Add the milk and mix until the dry ingredients are just moistened.

Flour a pastry board and roll out the dough to a 1cm thickness. Spread the ham and cheese on top and roll up the pastry. Place in refrigerator for approximately 30 minutes.

Slice the roll into rounds of about 1 cm thick. Bake for 15 minutes or until golden brown.

DRINKS

SLIMY PUNCH
1 packet green jelly
500 ml boiling water
500 ml apple juice
1 litre lemonade
ice cubes

Mix jelly powder with boiling water and add apple juice. Allow to cool before placing in refrigerator. Pour into a punch bowl and add the lemonade and ice cubes just before serving.
Serves 10.

DESSERT

ICE CREAM WITH LAVA
Scoop ice cream into bowls and pour over chocolate sauce and grated Crunchies.

You can buy chocolate sauce that sets on ice cream, or use the recipe given below.

CHOCOLATE SAUCE
200 g sugar
37,5 ml cocoa
pinch of salt
10 ml butter
75 ml boiling water
12,5 ml golden syrup
5 ml vanilla essence

Combine all the ingredients, except vanilla, in a saucepan. Bring to a boil while stirring to dissolve sugar. Remove from heat and add vanilla. Serve hot with ice cream.

Hamburger party

Every teenager loves hamburgers, even more so if he can prepare it himself. Patties can be prepared in advance and placed on the table alongside fresh bread rolls, tomato slices, cheese, onion and pineapple rings, lettuce leaves and two or three hamburger sauces. Ensure that there are at least two hamburger patties for each guest. Provide lots of snacks such as potato crisps, peanuts, raisins and popcorn. Make colourful Chinese lanterns for decorations or alternatively coloured lights always add to a cheerful atmosphere. Ice-cold gingerbeer goes down well in summer, while steaming mugs of milky coffee or hot chocolate are most welcome in winter. Ask the guests to wear their Cowboy gear – denim jeans, cowboy boots and Stetsons. Round off the theme by playing cheery Country-music.

MENU

Hamburgers with assorted sauces
Stuffed mushrooms
Potato salad or hot potato chips
Peach salad
Avocado dip
Quick gingerbeer
Cherry meringue cake
Easy peppermint tart

HAMBURGERS

HAMBURGER PATTIES
1 kg lean minced beef
2 chopped onions
2 slice of white bread, crumbed
2 eggs
salt and pepper
2 ml dried thyme
2 ml coriander

Mix all ingredients lightly with a fork. Roll out mixture between two layers of waxed paper to a thickness of about 2 cm.
Cut into circles measuring about 10 cm in diameter.
Makes 12 patties.

SAUCES

MUSHROOM CHEESE SAUCE
1 packet cream of mushroom soup powder
500 ml thick white sauce
100 g cheese, grated

Mix soup powder with white sauce over low heat and simmer for 2 minutes. Stir in cheese, remove from heat and serve hot.

PINEAPPLE MUSTARD SAUCE
1 x 820 g can crushed pineapple
30 ml soy sauce
125 ml mustard sauce

Combine pineapple, soy sauce and mustard sauce. Serve with pineapple rings.

MONKEYGLAND SAUCE
250 ml chutney
45 ml Worcestershire sauce
125 ml tomato sauce
1 ml Tabasco sauce

Combine all ingredients and serve in a small glass bowl.

SIDE DISH

STUFFED MUSHROOMS

6–8 black mushrooms
30 g fresh breadcrumbs
pinch of dried rosemary
½ onion, chopped
45 ml mayonnaise
5 ml Worcestershire sauce
salt and pepper
70 g Cheddar cheese, grated

Wipe mushrooms clean and remove stems. Chop stems finely and mix with breadcrumbs, rosemary, onion, mayonnaise, Worcestershire sauce, salt and pepper. Fill mushroom caps with the mixture. Arrange mushrooms on a greased baking sheet, sprinkle with cheese and grill until cheese is golden brown.
    Serves 6–8.

SALADS

POTATO SALAD

6 medium potatoes
1 large onion, chopped
2 hard-boiled eggs, sliced
10 ml salt
2 ml pepper
500 ml mayonnaise
12,5 ml chopped fresh parsley

Peel potatoes and boil until just soft, then slice or cube. Mix the potatoes lightly with the other ingredients.
For extra flavour, add one of more of the following:
• 60 ml chopped peanuts
• 50 ml chopped green pepper or dill cucumbers
• 50 ml crumbled, crispy bacon
    Serves 6–8.

• In stead of potato salad hot potato chips can be served. If you're pressed for time, buy frozen potato chips that can be prepared quickly and easily.

PEACH SALAD

1 x 410 g can peach halves, drained and chopped
10 cocktail onions
50 ml chopped nuts (optional)
Mayonnaise to serve

Combine all the ingredients and serve with mayonnaise.

DIPS

AVOCADO DIP

2 ripe avocados, mashed
12,5 ml lemon juice
5 ml salt
black pepper to taste
100 ml mayonnaise
10 ml grated onion

Combine all the ingredients and chill. Serve with crudités, potato crisps and crackers.

DRINKS

QUICK GINGERBEER

Delicious when prepared a few days in advance.

5 litres water
800 g sugar
10 ml Jamaican ginger
5 ml active dry yeast
10 ml cream of tartar
raisins

Bring water to the boil and add sugar, stirring to dissolve. Allow to cool until lukewarm. Add the remaining ingredients, except the raisins, and leave in a warm place for 12 hours to ferment.

Strain the mixture through a piece of muslin and pour into clean bottles. Add a few raisins to each bottle.

Replace the caps and leave to ferment for a few more hours at room temperature. Chill in refrigerator.

Enough for 25–30 glasses.

DESSERT

Teenagers do not always have a birthday cake, therefore special attention should be paid to the dessert. This cherry meringue tart will prove popular with the youngsters while the easy peppermint tart is quick to prepare and a proven success.

CHERRY MERINGUE CAKE

215 g cake flour
pinch of salt
2 ml ground cinnamon
60 g sugar
80 g almonds, finely chopped
125 g butter or margarine

FILLING

3 egg separated
80 g brown sugar
35 ml lemon juice
15 ml grated lemon rind
1 x 825 g can cherries, drained
150 ml strawberry jam
10 ml lemon juice
30 ml castor sugar
25 g slivered almonds

Preheat oven to 180°C. Sift flour, salt and cinnamon into a large bowl. Add sugar and almonds. Cut the butter into small cubes and rub into the dry ingredients until the mixture resembles fine breadcrumbs. Reserve 250 ml of the mixture and press the remainder onto the bottom and sides of a 23 cm spring-form cake tin. Bake for 15 minutes until golden brown. Allow to cool.

Beat the egg yolks, brown sugar, lemon juice and rind until light and fluffy. Cut up the cherries and arrange on pastry base. Pour the egg mixture evenly over cherries and sprinkle with the reserved crumb mixture. Bake for 20 minutes until lightly browned.

Mix the jam with the lemon juice. Spread over the cake as soon as it comes out of the oven. Add a pinch of salt to the egg whites and beat until foamy. Add the castor sugar gradually, beating continuously.

Spread the meringue mix over the warm cake, sprinkle with the slivered almonds and put back into the oven. Bake for a further 15 minutes until the meringue is light brown in colour.

Allow to cool for 25 minutes in the tin before removing. Serve with ice cream.

EASY PEPPERMINT TART

1 packet lime jelly powder
1 can (375 ml) evaporated milk, well chilled
50 ml castor sugar
1 packet Tennis biscuits
75 g butter or margarine, melted
1 small Peppermint Crisp

Dissolve jelly in one cup boiling water and allow to cool. Whip the evaporated milk and sugar until stiff. Stir jelly into milk mixture.

Crush the biscuits coarsely and mix with butter or margarine. Press the crumbs into a shallow pie plate and pour in the milk mixture. Leave to set in the refrigerator. Grate the Peppermint Crisp over tart and serve with cream or ice cream.

Pancake party

Sweet and savoury pancakes can make a meal fit for a king. They can be served in different ways: fold them twice and fill one of the 'pockets' with an interesting filling, or sprinkle with grated cheese and grill them in the oven. You can even make a pancake 'cake' by stacking a few pancakes on top of each other with different pie fillings in between. Refrigerate the fillings to set and cut it like an ordinary cake. Other snacks that tie in well with this theme are cold meats, cubed cheese, fruit and sausages. Savoury snacks like potato chips, nuts and crackers served with dips will whet the appetite and will be welcomed by those who may not be crazy about pancakes. Use a hot place to keep pancakes and fillings warm. In winter it is also advisable to warm the plates on which the pancakes are going to be served. Identify fillings with name tags to make it easier for guests to decide which filling they want.

PANCAKES

Prepare the batter a day in advance, but add the vinegar just before baking. The batter should be thin enough to cover the bottom of a pan easily when tilted.

800 g cake flour
10 ml salt
6 eggs
1 litre milk and 1 litre water or
2 litres water
200 ml sunflower oil
50 ml white vinegar

Sift dry ingredients together in a mixing bowl. Beat the eggs, milk, water and oil and gradually add to dry ingredients, beating well until the mixture is smooth.

Add the rest of the fluids and mix well. Bake in a very hot, greased pan.

Makes about 50 pancakes.

SAVOURY FILLINGS

A thick white sauce is the basis of most savoury fillings.

THICK WHITE SAUCE

45 ml butter or margarine
45 ml cake flour
1 ml salt
pinch of pepper
200 ml milk

Melt butter in a saucepan over low heat. Stir in the flour, salt and pepper until smooth. Add the milk

gradually, stirring continuously until the sauce is thick and glossy. Simmer for two minutes.

MUSHROOM FILLING

white sauce*
15 ml butter or margarine
1 onion, chopped
200 g mushrooms, chopped

Prepare the white sauce according to the recipe.

Sauté the onion and mushroom in butter or margarine. Add to white sauce and mix.

An easy alternative is to simply stir a packet of cream of mushroom soup into the white sauce.

SEAFOOD FILLING

white sauce*
1 onion, chopped
15 ml butter or margarine
250 g cooked or canned mixed seafood, mussels, tuna, shrimps and fish
salt and pepper

Prepare the white sauce according to the recipe. Sauté the onion in the butter or margarine, add seafood, season with salt and pepper and sauté briefly. Stir into the white sauce and mix well.

HAM FILLING

white sauce*
250 g ham, chopped
1 x 200g canned mushrooms

Prepare the white sauce according to the recipe. Add the ham and mushrooms and simmer until heated through.

MEAT FILLING

Use cooked mince and flavour with onion and tomato.

CHICKEN FILLING

Thicken leftover chicken with chicken or mushroom soup.

SWEET FILLINGS

Pancakes sprinkled with cinnamon-sugar and lemon juice and served with cream or ice-cream is a classic dessert. The following fillings are delicious alternatives (enough for 8–12 pancakes) and can also be served with cream or ice cream.

BANANA FILLING
30 ml butter or margarine
6 bananas, mashed
20 ml lemon juice
20 ml honey or golden syrup
100 g blanched almonds, chopped

Melt the butter or margarine in a frying pan and add the remaining ingredients. Fry lightly and fill pancakes with the mixture.

CHEESE AND ORANGE FILLING
125 g cottage cheese
100 g walnuts, chopped
20 ml sugar
1 egg
5 ml grated orange rind

ORANGE SAUCE
200 g sugar
125 ml orange juice
50 ml butter or margarine
5 ml grated orange rind
15 ml lemon juice

Preheat oven to 180°C. Mix all the ingredients for the filling and spoon onto pancakes.

Make the sauce by heating ingredients over low heat until sugar is dissolved. Remove the pan from the heat as soon as it starts boiling rapidly.

Pour the sauce over the pancakes and bake for 15 minutes. Serve hot with cream or ice cream.

STRAWBERRY/CHERRY FILLING
25 ml butter or margarine
120 g sugar
125 ml orange juice
25 ml brandy
250 g hulled strawberries or stoned cherries

Melt the butter or margarine, add the sugar, orange juice and brandy and stir over low heat until sugar is dissolved. Boil for 5 minutes then add halved strawberries or cherries and mix gently until fruit is covered in sauce.

DESSERT

COFFEE CAKE

25 g butter or margarine
170 g sugar
40 ml golden syrup
2 eggs
260 g cake flour
12,5 ml baking powder
pinch of salt
5 ml ground cinnamon
15 ml instant coffee powder
125 ml water
125 ml milk
walnuts to decorate

ICING

75 g butter or margarine
175 g icing sugar
10 ml instant coffee powder
15 ml cocoa
5 ml vanilla essence
15 ml water

Preheat oven to 180°C. Grease two 20 cm round cake tins. Cream the butter or margarine and sugar, add golden syrup and beat well.

Add the eggs one at a time, beating well after each addition. Sift the flour, baking powder, salt and cinnamon together.

Dissolve the coffee powder in the water and add alternately with the milk to the dry ingredients. Mix lightly.

Divide the mixture between the two tins and bake for 35–40 minutes. Turn out onto a wire rack and allow to cool.

Make the icing by mixing all the ingredients, except the walnuts, well.

Spread half the icing onto one cake, top with the second cake and spread with the remaining icing. Decorate with walnuts.

PANCAKE CAKE

10–15 pancakes
1 litre thick custard
pie fillings in different flavours

Line a spring-form cake tin with wax paper. Place a pancake on the bottom of the tin. Spread a layer of custard over. Place another pancake onto the custard. Spread a layer of pie filling over. Place a pancake on top. Repeat the steps until the cake is high enough.

Refrigerate overnight. Remove from the refrigerator, just before serving and decorate with whipped cream. Slice like a layered cake (see photo).

DRINKS

MOCHA DRINK

50 ml cocoa
2,5 litres milk
20 ml instant coffee powder
125 ml sugar
chocolate vermicelli

Place all ingredients in blender and blend well. Pour into mugs and sprinkle with vermicelli.
Serves 8.

Pizza Party

Surely there isn't a child who doesn't enjoy pizza? It makes a very popular theme for a party. Pizzas are relatively inexpensive and very filling for hungry pre-teens. Present the party in the form of a Mafia-gathering. Invitations should request guests to dress accordingly. Award a prize to the best-dressed 'gangster'.
Prepare a few large pizzas with different toppings in advance, and cut them into slices so that each guest can taste all the toppings. Alternatively, let them choose their own toppings to create original individual pizzas. Ensure that you have enough space to cook all the pizzas simultaneously, should you decide on the last option.

MENU

Pizzas
Tomato and mozzarella salad
Pasta salad
Mafia brew
Cassata
Toffee chocolate cake

PIZZAS

BASIC PIZZA DOUGH
325 g cake flour
15 ml sugar
10 g dry yeast
5 ml salt
15 ml butter or margarine
125 ml lukewarm water
125 ml lukewarm milk

Preheat oven to 200°C. Mix the flour, sugar, dry yeast and salt in a large mixing bowl. Rub the butter or margarine into the dry ingredients, add water and milk and knead to a soft, smooth dough. Cover the dough and leave to rise for 10 minutes in a warm place.

Halve the dough and roll out into two 23 cm-diameter circles. Leave in a warm place until the dough has doubled in volume.

Spread with pizza base sauce*. Arrange toppings on base as desired and bake for 20–25 minutes or until base is cooked.

Makes two medium pizzas.

QUICK PIZZA DOUGH
250 g self-raising flour
150 ml boiling water
100 ml oil
pinch of salt

Place all the ingredients in a container with a lid and shake until a soft dough has formed. Refrigerate until firm, then roll out as required.

Bake for 10 minutes before adding toppings. Spread with pizza base sauce* and follow with desired toppings. Bake for a further 5 minutes.

Makes two medium pizzas.

COTTAGE CHEESE PIZZA DOUGH
250 g smooth cottage cheese
150 ml milk
150 ml oil
5 ml salt
500 g cake flour
5 ml baking powder

Preheat oven to 200°C. Mix the cottage cheese, oil, milk, salt and half of the flour well. Sift the remaining flour and baking powder over and knead to a firm dough. Refrigerate overnight and roll out to fit a greased baking tray. Spread dough with pizza base sauce* and follow with desired toppings. Bake for 40 minutes.

Makes one large or two medium pizzas.

PIZZA BASE SAUCE

1 onion, chopped
½ celery stick, chopped
30 ml olive oil
2 x 410 g cans tomatoes
5 ml dried basil
1 bay leaf
5 ml sugar
30 ml tomato paste
5 ml salt
freshly ground black pepper

Sauté onion and celery in hot oil until translucent. Add remaining ingredients and simmer, uncovered, for 45–60 minutes until thick. Remove bay leaf.

Makes about 500ml sauce.

CLASSIC PIZZA TOPPINGS

- Ham, salami or bacon
- Sliced smoked or cooked sausage
- Mushrooms, green pepper, onion, spring onions, tomatoes
- Olives, asparagus, sweetcorn
- Anchovies, tuna, mussels, calamari, shrimps
- Banana, pineapple
- Fried or boiled eggs
- Feta, Gorgonzola, Mozzarella, or Cheddar cheese

ECONOMICAL BREAD PIZZA

1 large onion, sliced
15 ml oil
12–14 thin slices white bread,
crusts removed and quartered
6 rashers of bacon, crisply fried
and chopped
200 g Cheddar cheese, grated
500 ml milk
7 large eggs, beaten
7,5 ml mustard powder
2 ml paprika
5 ml salt
1 ml pepper

Preheat oven to 180°C, Sauté onion in oil until soft and translucent. Place a single layer of bread in a 20 cm-square greased casserole. Sprinkle with the onion, bacon and half the cheese. Repeat the layers until all the ingredients have been used.

Beat the milk, eggs and seasoning together. Pour over bread and bake for 35–45 minutes, or until set and golden brown.

Serves 6–8.

MINI PIZZAS

120 g cake flour
2,5 ml baking powder
1 ml of salt
60 ml butter or margarine
5 ml lemon juice
30 ml ice water
tomato slices
Cheddar or Mozzerella cheese

Preheat oven to 200°C. Sift dry ingredients together. Cut butter or margarine into flour mixture.

Mix lemon juice and water and sprinkle evenly over mixture. Mix lightly with a fork and then with your hands to form a ball. Handle as little as possible.

Chill dough, then roll out. Cut into small circles with cookie cutter. Place a slice of tomato and some grated cheese on each circle.

Bake for about 20 minutes or until dough is cooked.

Makes 10 mini pizzas.

DRINKS

Mafia brew

2 litres Coca-Cola or Crème Soda
1 litre chocolate ice cream

Fill each glass two thirds with soda of your choice. Spoon ice cream on top. Leave for about 1 minute and serve with straws and parfait spoons.

Serves 10.

SALADS

TOMATO AND MOZZARELLA SALAD

6 Mediterranean tomatoes
180 g Mozzarella cheese
salt and freshly ground black pepper
chopped basil

Slice off the top of the tomatoes and hollow out using a grapefruit spoon. Sprinkle with salt and pepper. Make Mozzarella balls with a melon-baller.

Place a Mozzarella ball into each tomato and garnish with basil.

Makes 6.

PASTA SALAD

200 g pasta, cooked
200 g Cheddar cheese, cubed
250 g cooked ham, cubed
100 g fresh peas

1 red pepper, chopped
125 ml mayonnaise
salt and pepper to taste

Mix all the ingredients together lightly, season and serve with bread sticks.

DESSERT

QUICK CASSATA

1 litre vanilla ice cream
150 g each red and green glacé cherries
100 g nuts, chopped

Allow ice cream to soften slightly, then mix in the cherries and nuts. Spoon into mini bread tins and freeze.

Remove from freezer just before serving. Turn out onto side plates and garnish with sprigs of mint.

Serves 6–8.

TOFFEE CHOCOLATE CAKE

125 g butter or margarine
125 g brown sugar
2 eggs
175 g self-raising flour
70 g ground almonds
75 g dark chocolate, grated

ICING

60 g butter or margarine
125 g brown sugar
30 ml golden syrup
125 ml cream
Flakes to decorate (optional)

Preheat oven to 180°C. Grease a 20 cm round cake tin and line with greaseproof paper.

Cream butter and sugar until light and fluffy. Add eggs one at a time, beating well after each addition. Fold in flour, almonds and grated chocolate. Pour into cake tin and bake for 1/ hour until firm.

Make the icing by heating the butter, sugar and syrup together in a saucepan over low heat, stirring until sugar has dissolved.

Heat mixture to boiling point, lower heat immediately and simmer, without stirring, for 5 minutes. Remove from heat and add cream gradually, beating well with a wooden spoon. Put aside to cool and thicken.

Spread icing over cake and decorate with chocolate Flakes, if desired.

Around the fondue pot

This party is most suited to older teenagers when both sexes are invited. It's important to keep the guest list short; limit it to six guests per fondue pot. For a cheese fondue the sauce is prepared in advance and poured into the fondue pot just before the guests arrive. A variety of snacks can be served with this sauce for instance, cubed French loaf and vegetables. If you choose to serve meat, hot bouillon can be used as an alternative to oil. Dips are always very popular and can be served before or during the meal with potato crisps and savoury biscuits. A crisp green salad can also be served. A chocolate fondue is a perfect dessert, served with cubes of cake, marshmallows, or fruit.
Fruit punch goes well with a cheese fondue.

MENU

Cheese fondue
Mixed salad
Fruit punch
Chocolate fondue

CHEESE FONDUE

CHEESE SAUCE 1

1 kg mature Cheddar cheese
50 ml cake flour
500 ml apple juice
25 ml butter or margarine
5 ml mustard powder
salt and pepper

Grate cheese coarsely and sprinkle with flour to coat lightly. Heat apple juice to just below boiling point. Add one third of the cheese and flour mixture and stir briskly with a wooden spoon. Do not boil.

As soon as the cheese has melted, add the rest of the cheese, one third at a time, stirring briskly. Stir in butter or margarine, mustard powder, and seasoning.

Transfer to a fondue pot and place on the burner

NOTE: The flame should be very low and the sauce should never boil, as this will cause it to curdle.

CHEESE SAUCE 2

285 ml milk
400 g Gouda cheese, grated
10 ml cornflour
5 ml mustard powder
30 ml water
10 ml Worcestershire sauce
salt
freshly ground black pepper

Place the milk in a fondue pot and slowly bring to the boil over moderate heat. Reduce the heat and stir in the grated cheese.

Blend the cornflour and mustard with water to form a smooth paste and stir into cheese mixture. Stir in the Worcestershire sauce and seasoning.

Continue stirring the hot sauce until it is thoroughly blended and smooth. Serve immediately.

Both sauces serve 6–8.

The following can be dipped in the cheese fondue:
• Cubes of bread, savoury biscuits
• Cooked meatballs, smoked sausages, cubed ham
• Cubed pieces of fresh fruit, such as pineapple and banana or dried apple rings and prunes
• Freshly chopped vegetables such as cauliflower, broccoli, carrots, cocktail tomatoes, green beans, celery and gherkins are very colourful and a very healthy addition to the meal.

DIPS

PARTY DIP
100 ml mayonnaise
50 ml tomato sauce
30 ml Worcestershire sauce
12,5 ml grated onion
250 g cream- or cottage cheese

Mix together all ingredients and chill. Garnish with parsley and serve with potato crisps, crackers and crudités.

BILTONG DIP
30 ml oil
2 spring onions, chopped
250 g button mushrooms
250 ml mayonnaise
125 ml sour cream
salt and pepper to taste
250 ml grated biltong

Heat oil and sauté the onion and mushrooms. Place in a food processor or blender with the mayonnaise, sour cream, salt and pepper and blend until smooth. Add the biltong and mix well.

BANANA DIP
3 bananas, mashed
100 g smooth cream- or cottage cheese
3 ml celery salt
12,5 ml chutney
12,5 ml lemon juice
20 ml orange juice

Mix all the ingredients thoroughly and leave to stand for an hour to allow the flavour to develop. Serve with potato crisps and crackers.

YOGHURT AND HONEY DIP
250 ml natural yoghurt
45 ml orange juice
15 ml honey
15 ml lemon juice
15 ml chopped, fresh mint
2 ml salt
freshly ground black pepper to taste

Mix all ingredients together and serve with a selection of fresh fruit, such as pineapple cubes, melon balls, apple, pear and orange segments.

SAUCES FOR MEAT FONDUE

The following sauces will be enjoyed by everyone, should you decide on a meat fondue. Cut the meat into small cubes, cook in hot bouillon or oil and then dip into one of the sauces.

TOMATO SAUCE
12,5 ml oil
1 small onion, chopped
250 g tomatoes
1 clove garlic, crushed
2 ml salt
dash of pepper
30 ml chopped fresh parsley

Heat oil and sauté onion until softened. Skin tomatoes, chop and add to onion. Add garlic, salt and pepper and simmer until the sauce is thick and most of the liquid has evaporated. Stir in parsley and serve.

MUSTARD SAUCE
200 ml evaporated milk
30 ml mustard powder
1 onion, chopped
10 ml sugar
3 ml salt

Combine ingredients, heat gently and serve hot.

AVOCADO SAUCE
1 ripe avocado
15 ml lemon juice
30 ml cream
15 ml chopped green pepper
freshly ground black pepper to taste

Mash the avocado and combine with the remaining ingredients.

DRINKS

FRUIT PUNCH
750 ml lime concentrate
113 g granadilla pulp
250 ml fresh orange juice
50 ml lemon juice
250 g crushed pineapple
500 ml lemonade
500 ml ginger ale
1 litre soda water

Mix together all the ingredients, except lemonade, ginger ale and soda water.

Chill in refrigerator. Pour mixture into a large punch bowl and stir in remaining ingredients, just before serving.

Makes about 15–20 glasses.

CHOCOLATE FONDUE

CHOCOLATE SAUCE
200 g sugar
45 ml cocoa
pinch of salt
10 ml butter
125 ml boiling water
25 ml golden syrup
5 ml vanilla essence

Place all ingredients, except vanilla, in a saucepan. Bring to the boil, stirring to dissolve the sugar. Remove from the heat as soon as the mixture boils. Stir in the vanilla and keep warm on the burner.

QUICK CHOCOLATE SAUCE
Melt a large block of milk chocolate over simmering water. Add 250 ml cream, stir until smooth.

ORANGE CHOCOLATE SAUCE
100 g chocolate with raisins
100 g dark chocolate
5 ml grated orange rind
130 ml orange or apricot juice
2 egg yolks
5 ml rum essence

Melt chocolate in a double boiler and add the orange rind and fruit juice, stirring continuously. Do not allow the mixture to boil.

Beat egg yolks lightly, stir in a little of the chocolate mixture, then add to chocolate mixture together with rum essence. Stir well. Pour the mixture into a fondue pot and keep warm over a low burner.

The following can be dipped in the chocolate sauce:
- Cubes of sponge cake, crisp biscuits and cookies, marshmallows
- Strawberries, sliced banana, kiwi fruit and other cubed fruit

Provide bowls with sprinkle nuts or desiccated coconut on the table.

Games & entertainment

Decide well in advance which games and activities are going to be played. In fine weather the older ones will usually keep themselves amused, but if it's pouring outside, or the children don't know each other, a few games will keep everybody happy and occupied. It is important that the children invited are all of the same age, otherwise it becomes an impossible task to arrange suitable activities. To make the choice of games easier, they have been grouped according to age groups: one to two years; three to five years; six to eight years; and nine to eleven years. Older children prefer being left to their own devices – as long as the music is good, they'll be happy!

1–2 YEARS

At this age babies find it difficult to socialise and can't participate in group activities. The best way of keeping them occupied is by ensuring that everyone has something to play with. Ask mothers to bring along their child's favourite toy, as well as a walking ring where appropriate.

Babies love tearing paper – give them inexpensive crinkle or other soft paper that won't cut their hands.

Fill large ice cream containers with a variety of well-known objects, then let them empty out the contents on the carpet and put everything back in the containers again.

A sandpit is ideal for a hot summer's day, but keep an eye on them as they're inclined either to eat the sand or throw it at each other.

BLOWING BUBBLES

Give each child a mug one-third full of an inexpensive soapy mixture. Loop a piece of wire at one end and let them blow bubbles.

MAKING MUSIC

If you can stand the din, give each child a saucepan or plastic bowl and a few spoons.

CARDBOARD BOXES

Large cardboard boxes will keep this age group occupied for a long time.

Give them each one (the children should be able to fit in them) and soon the boxes will be transformed into trains, cars and any other toy you can think of.

Play dough

Make play dough in different colours and give each little one a few pieces. Let everyone work on a tray or wooden plank. The clay is totally harmless and, because it contains so much salt, is not likely to be eaten.

240 g cake flour
500 ml water
200 g salt
20 ml cream of tartar
15 ml oil
15 ml food colouring

Heat all ingredients over very low heat until mixture becomes sticky. Remove from stove and knead for 1 minute.

Add more flour if mixture is too soft. Store in an airtight container.

3 – 5 YEARS

Toddlers are a difficult group to keep occupied. They get bored very easily and are difficult to organise.

Group games should be kept simple and not be too rough. Any music game, where the children can hold hands and move in a circle, is a good choice.

You will have to be patient to let everything run smoothly.

Tower of Pisa
You need
Square building blocks

To Play
One child starts building a tower while the others take turns in throwing a dice. The first one to throw a six flattens the tower and then starts building it himself.

The first one to complete the tower, using all the blocks, before someone else throws a six, is the winner. The older the children are, the more blocks there should be.

Thread the ring
You need
A long, thin piece of string and a ring or large button. The ring should not be too large as the children have to be able to hide it in their hands.

To Play
Let the children sit in a circle. Thread the string through the ring or large button and knot the ends so as to form a circle as large as the circle of children. All the children hold onto the string with both hands, pretending to slide the ring along the string. One child stands in the middle and tries to spot who has the ring. If he's right, the one caught stands in the middle.

Puppet show or video
If it's very cold or raining, a puppet show is ideal for this age group but keep it as simple as possible and you'll have them rolling on the floor. Another alternative is showing an animated video or cartoon. Parties for this age group never carry on for too long, and before you know it the afternoon has come to an end.

PASS THE PRESENT

YOU NEED

Small gifts such as cars, dolls or plastic jewellery, and brightly coloured wrapping paper or newspaper. You'll need adhesive tape and small sweets, such as Smarties or Jelly tots.

TO PLAY

Wrap a small gift in several layers of wrapping paper or newspaper. Secure each layer with sticky tape and hide small sweets in the wrapping to add interest. Let the children sit in a circle. While the music is playing, the children pass the gift around; when the music stops, the one holding the present must strip off a layer of the paper and pass it on again when the music restarts. The one who takes off the last layer, wins the present.

STOP THE MUSIC!

YOU NEED

A CD player and some lively music. This game can be played in various ways – use your imagination! A few examples are given below.

TO PLAY

- Let the children jump up and down while you play music. As soon as the music stops, everybody sits down. The last one to sit is out. Carry on until there is only one child left in the game.
- Let everyone jump around or run in a circle. When the music stops, everyone freezes. The one who moves first is out, and the winner is once again the one who remains.
- Let everyone sit in a circle and pass around an old hat, or anything they can put on their heads. Each child has to put the hat on his or her head before passing it on. When the music stops, the one with the hat on his head is out.
- Let the two tallest children form an arch with their arms. With the music playing, the other children then run through the arch. When the music stops, the one caught in the arch stands behind either one of those forming the arch. Continue until there is only one child left.

PARTY BEE BOXES

YOU NEED

Empty toilet roll, yellow serviette, pipe cleaners, black and yellow paint.

Prepare everything beforehand and let the toddlers assemble and fill their party bee boxes with sweets to take home. Using empty toilet paper rolls. Make an incision on either side of each roll. Push a yellow serviette or crinkle paper through the incisions to form the wings as shown. Use pipe cleaners for feelers and yellow and black paint or crayons for the stripes.

FIND THE SWEETS

This age group enjoy searching for hidden treats. Hide a few sweets or other goodies in the room and tell everyone to hunt for them. If anyone finds something he has to stand still and eat it before looking for more. Wrappers must be kept as proof and the one who has the most after a few minutes, receives a small prize.

INSECT ANTICS

Give every child the opportunity to choose an insect and, without telling the other children, to perform a few actions that will enable the others to guess which insect was chosen.

The child who guesses correctly takes a turn at being an insect. Let the birthday child start the game and make sure that each child gets a turn to be on centre stage, but don't pressurise the shy ones.

WOLF, WOLF, WHAT'S THE TIME?

This is one of the traditional favourites. One child is the wolf while the rest follow him, chanting 'Wolf, Wolf, what's the time?' They're quite safe until the wolf says '12 o'clock, lunchtime!'. The children must scatter, as the one who is caught has to take the wolf's place.

FUNNY FACES

Everyone sits in a circle. The birthday child pulls a funny face; the child sitting next to him has to copy him and change the funny face slightly. The next child has to continue the game and so on.

The hard part is that no one may laugh and everybody has to keep his or her funny face intact!

BLOW THE BALLOON

The children hold hands and form a circle. Throw a balloon into the centre of the circle.

Everybody has to try to keep the balloon in the air by blowing at it. They must keep holding hands. If there are many children, divide them into smaller groups to make the game easier.

6 – 8 YEARS

This is a very energetic age group and your planning will have to be thorough if everyone is to be kept occupied! These children love playing games and fortunately the number of games suitable for this age group is almost unlimited.

CRAWLING ANTS

This game is based on the ever popular 'I wrote a letter to my love'. The children sit in a circle while one runs behind them with a handkerchief in his hands. While he is running, the children close their eyes and sing a rhyme. When they sing the last line, he drops the handkerchief behind someone's back. This person then jumps up and tries to catch him before he can sit in the place left vacant.

RHYME

A little ant came crawling by
he found a crumb but my oh my
the crumb was dropped
the ant has stopped
who'll be the next ant
crawling by?

COPS AND ROBBERS

Divide the partygoers into two groups – cops and robbers, with the robbers wearing masks to identify them. The purpose is to either catch all the robbers or to shoot all the policemen. Each group has a 'safe' area where the other group may not catch them. A thief shoots a policeman by catching him and branding him on the forehead with a blackened piece of cork. Being 'shot', the policeman is out of the game. Thieves have to be caught and unmasked. They are also then out of the game. The group succeeding in catching or shooting all the members of the other group first, is the winner.

TEN LITTLE ELVES

Divide the children into two groups. Draw two parallel lines about 10 metres apart. Group A must choose what to depict and then go to Group B and say:

Group A: Ten little elves are looking for work!
Group B: What kind of work?
Group A: Any work!
Group B: Show us what you can do.

Group A then act out their charade, for example fishing or picking apples. Group B has to guess what they're doing. If they get it right, Group A run away and Group B has to catch them. Those caught have to join Group B.

Group B then has a turn acting out a charade. The winning team is the one with the most members at the end of the game.

GRAB-A-TREASURE
YOU NEED
A 'treasure chest' full of small gifts. The chest can be made of an old shoebox covered with foil or other shiny paper. You can fill it with practically anything, from small gifts, such as sweets, small cars or plastic animals to more valuable gifts to make things more exciting.

TO PLAY
The children sit in a circle on chairs or on the floor. While the music is playing, the treasure box is passed around. When the music stops, the person holding the box has to grab a 'treasure' from the box without looking and then passes the box on again. Repeat until each child has at least one gift to take home.

TREASURE HUNT 1
YOU NEED
A gift for each child which he has to hunt for himself. Fill matchboxes or small jewellery boxes with small gifts or chocolate coins (a real coin could also be included). Wrap the boxes in pretty paper and mark each one with a number or symbol, such as a red triangle. Devise a clue for every treasure and place the clues in a hat. Everyone then draws a clue and looks for his or her treasure. Example of a clue: 'look for the red triangle close to the tree with the purple flowers. Hope you find it soon! From Long John Silver'.

TO PLAY
Before the party, write the clues and hide the treasures accordingly. Be careful not to make the clues too difficult – the children might just give up hope and abandon the game. Every child gets a turn to retrieve a clue from the hat and then go and look for the treasure. Help those who don't find their treasure relatively quickly.

TREASURE HUNT 2
YOU NEED
Small wrapped presents in a large box that is also filled with bunched-up newspaper or straw.

TO PLAY
Blindfold the children and let them hunt for the treasure amongst the newspaper or straw. Allow only a few minutes per child. The other children could sing a song or recite a rhyme at the end of which time would be up.

RHYME
Long John Silver find your
treasure,
You thought you were oh
so clever
It's hidden now, but soon
you'll find
A beautiful gift of the rarest kind

FOLLOW-MY-LEADER
A child known for originality and a sense of humour is chosen as leader. The leader sets off at a brisk pace and the rest, following in single file, copy his actions.

The leader has to vary his antics constantly and the more humorous, the better. He could walk on all fours, touch his toes, run a few yards backwards, spin around and so on.

When everybody is tired, the leader can sit on the grass so that all can rest. This is the ideal time to bring out the snacks!

Vary the leaders regularly, but don't force the role on anybody who protests too much. Some children are genuinely shy and would far rather follow than lead.

HOT POTATO
A fun game to play indoors when the weather isn't favourable for outdoor activities.

While the others aren't looking, one person hides something, such as a ball or handkerchief. The other then have to try and find the article.

As soon as someone is close the person who hid the article says 'lukewarm', 'hot' or 'very hot' as the case may be. However, he doesn't have to say which person is close to the hidden article!

The child who finds the article gets to hide it next.

FASHION PARADE

Borrow as many old clothes, shoes, handbags, lipsticks, nail varnish and jewellery as you can. Clear a room and place all you have collected in it.

Give each child a hanger for her own clothes and let her choose a new outfit. Have a fashion parade with a small prize for the person with the most original outfit. To ensure that no one is left out, create categories such as 'the lady with the pretties hat' or 'the most colourful combination' and hand out prizes to them as well.

Make certain that everyone is a winner.

CRABS, CROWS AND CRAYFISH

Divide the children into two groups to form two rows next to each other: the 'crows' and the 'crabs'.

One person stands in front of the rows and calls loudly: 'C-r-r-rabs' or 'c-r-r-rows' or 'c-r-r-rayfish'. On hearing 'crabs', the crabs run away with the crows giving chase. If a crab is caught, he becomes a crow. If the call is 'crows', the crows run away, this time with the crabs in pursuit. If 'crayfish' is called, both groups freeze. Any person who moves, or starts to run, must join the other group.

After a while the groups are counted and the largest group is the winner.

TRAFFIC TEST

YOU NEED
The basic traffic signs that children should know at this age.

TO PLAY
The hostess or other adult pretends to be a traffic officer and in a fun way asks the children what certain road signs mean. Correct answers are rewarded with something small, such as a sweet.

This is a novel way of teaching children about road safety – while they're having fun!

DRESSING UP

YOU NEED
A large box filled with old clothes of all shapes and sizes – gloves, hats, pyjamas, scarves, and so on.

TO PLAY
If there are ten children, place nine articles in a box in the corner of the room.

When a whistle is blown, the children rush over to the box and put on an article of clothing.

The child who doesn't find anything is out of the game and then helps you put eight articles in the box.

With each round an article of clothing is simply put on over the others. Each time, one less article of clothing is placed in the box until only one child remains who by now is wearing ten different items of clothing!

WHAT'S DIFFERENT?

This is an ideal indoor game. Two children leave the room and put on other, or each other's clothes. When they come back, the others have to guess what's different.

WHISPERS

The children sit in a circle and the birthday child whispers something to his neighbour. He in turn repeats whatever he heard to the child next to him. The message is repeated all round the circle. The last child in the circle then says aloud what he heard, which seldom bears any relation to the original whispered message!

FIND YOUR MATE

YOU NEED
Several pieces of paper in two different colours (e.g. red and blue), and safety pins to pin the paper to the children's clothing.

TO PLAY
Print half the name of an animal on a red piece of paper, and the

other half on a blue piece, for example ELE on red paper and PHANT on blue. Other examples would be MON and KEY or BUTTER and FLY.

Divide the children into two groups and pin the red pieces of paper onto the backs of one group and the blue onto the second group.

When the two groups meet, they ask questions such as: 'What colour are you?' or 'Am I spotted or striped'. The first couple to find each other are the winners.

9 – 10 YEARS

This very enthusiastic age group is often the easiest to entertain. Competitive games are very popular, but alternate rowdy games with quieter ones. Because boys of this age can be quite wild and rough, their games will need a bit of organising.

FIND YOUR PARTNER

This is a good game if there are boys as well as girls. It is often a nice ice-breaker, especially if they are somewhat shy to begin with.

Write two names that are normally associated with one another on a piece of paper, i.e. Romeo and Juliet, salt and pepper, bacon and eggs.

The papers are cut in half, one half jumbled and given to the boys and the other to the girls. Blow a whistle to indicate the start of the game and give them sixty seconds to find their partners.

EATING CHOCOLATE
YOU NEED
A slab of chocolate on a plate, a knife and fork, hat, coat, scarf, a pair of gloves and a dice.

TO PLAY
The youngsters sit in a circle, taking turns to throw the dice. Any one throwing a six must get up, put on the coat, hat, gloves and scarf and try to eat as much chocolate as possible using a knife and fork.

Meanwhile, the others continue throwing the dice. If someone else throws a six, the previous chocolate-eater immediately hands over the coat, hat, scarf and gloves to the newcomer who then proceeds to tackle the chocolate with the knife and fork.

Everyone will be laughing so much that the chocolate will be virtually untouched.

UNROLL THE TOILET PAPER
This game is a lot of fun, but also quite taxing for the participants!

Divide the youngsters into groups of four to six. Each group forms a line and is given a roll of toilet paper.

The person in front holds on to the end of the toilet paper and passes the toilet roll over his head to the person standing behind him.

When the last person in the line receives the roll, he passes the roll between his legs to the person in front of him until the roll reaches the first person again. The teams continue in this way, with the roll

passing to and fro, until all the paper has been used. Then, still without breaking the paper, the teams have to walk about ten metres to the winning post. The first team home is the winner.

NOTE: If the toilet paper breaks, that team falls out!

BLOW THE BALL
YOU NEED
A tennis ball, old table top and chalk.

TO PLAY
Divide the youngsters into two teams and seat them on opposite sides of a table.

Chalk in a centre line and goal posts on the table. One team 'kicks off' – and to score, they have to blow a table tennis ball between the goal posts.

If someone blows the ball off the table, he falls out and the other team 'kicks off'. The winning team is declared after ten minutes.

HIGHWAYMAN

Youngsters form a circle, with a blindfolded 'highwayman' in the centre. Everyone in the circle receives a number and then changes places.

The highwayman calls: 'The mail-coach leaves at five to eight!' Number five and eight must follow the shortest route within the circle to change places with each other while the highwayman tries to catch one of them.

If he succeeds, he changes places with that person. If he doesn't he calls out two other numbers.

To give the highwayman a fair chance, the circle shouldn't be big.

ROLLER-BALL

This is an exiting game in which every participant gets a chance to score.

YOU NEED

Five fairly large brown paper bags, a wall and a tennis ball.

TO PLAY

Inflate the paper bags and seal. Place them in a row on the floor, about 30 cm apart and one metre from the wall.

The knack is to roll the tennis ball against the wall in such a way that it knocks over a paper bag as it rolls back. Participants are allowed five throws per turn. The player who manages to knock over the most bags is the winner.

AND THEN...

The birthday child starts telling a story, such as: 'One day there was an old man with only one eye...', and the person next to him takes up the story. You decide when a story is long enough and when the next person should continue.

ELLY ROSE

Each boy takes a girl as partner and they form two lines – boys in one line and girls in another. A 'widower' stands with his back to them and calls 'Elly Rose!'

The couple at the back run to the front on opposite sides of the rows. Without breaking up the rows, the widower and the boy try to catch the girl.

The one who succeeds becomes the girl's partner and falls in line, and the other one becomes the widower.

If there are more girls than boys, let a girl be 'widow'.

DONKEY

Youngsters stand in a circle and the birthday child gives each a number. He then throws a ball in the air and calls a number.

The person with the corresponding number runs forward and tries to catch the ball. If he succeeds, he immediately throws the ball in the air and calls another number.

If he misses, he tries to get hold of the ball as quickly as possible while the others try to run way as far as they can. As soon as he gets hold of the ball, he shouts: 'Stop!' and everybody freezes.

Now the fun starts: the person holding the ball gives orders to anyone moving, such as 'Spell your name in giant steps towards me' or 'Spell your name and surname in baby steps towards me', which they then have to do.

As soon as all those who moved, have been 'punished', the person with the ball throws the ball at the nearest person.

If he misses, he is given the first letter of the word 'Donkey', but if he hits the person, that person is given the 'D'.

The person at whom the ball was thrown, whether he was hit or not, grabs the ball, throws it in the air and calls a number.

The game continues in this way until one participant has been caught so many times that he has all the letters of the word 'donkey'.

Basic Recipes

All the birthday cakes are baked according to a basic recipe, which is simply adapted for different sizes. Other basic recipes used throughout are butter icing and royal icing. Pastry cases are very handy, especially if baked in small patty pans. The size is just right so that they can be handled with ease. They can be filled with a sweet or savoury filling, but do remember to fill them on the day of the party, as they tend to become soggy if filled days in advance. Meringues are always a favourite – they can be tinted a delicate shade with food colouring and served plain or with a filling. Meringue mixture can be shaped and used in many different ways to make meringue nests, hearts and other interesting decorations.

METRIC CONVERSION TABLE

MEASURING JUG	TABLESPOON	TEASPOON
¼ cup = 60 ml	1 T = 15 ml	¼ t = 1 ml
½ cup = 125 ml	2 T = 30 ml	½ t = 3 ml
¾ cup = 180 ml	3 T = 45 ml	1 t = 5 ml
1 cup = 250 ml	4 T = 60 ml	2 t = 10 ml
2 cup = 500 ml		3 t = 15 ml
		4 t = 20 ml

NOTE

In many of the recipes in this book, the measurements and quantities have been left out. This is done purposely, as quantities will largely depend on the number of guests. The success of these recipes does not depend on precise amounts or measurements, but rather on your imagination. Basic recipes used elsewhere in the book have been marked with an asterisk.

QUICK CAKE BAKING TIME

SIZE	TIME	
2 x round cake tin (20 cm)	30 min	35 min
1 x square/round cake tin (25 cm)	45 min	50 min
1 x rectangular cake tin (21 cm x 26 cm)	40 min	45 min
1 x bread tin (12cm x 22cm)	35 min	35 min
Large cup cakes	15 min	15 min

QUICK CAKE MIX

This recipe is most suitable for birthday cakes as the cake keeps well – up to a week in a tin and up to two weeks if decorated. It is soft and moist, yet firm enough to slice easily. Use an electric knife to make the cutting even easier. Just remember not to press down but to allow the knife to simply glide through the cake.

QUICK CAKE MIX: SIZE 1
240 g self-raising flour
200 g castor sugar
pinch of salt
125 g butter or margarine (soft or cut in blocks)
2 eggs
125 ml milk
5 m vanilla essence

Preheat the oven to 180°C and spray the cake tins with non-stick baking spray or butter the tins and sprinkle with flour, shaking out the excess. Place all the ingredients in a mixing bowl and mix, first with a wooden spoon and then with a hand-mixer for 1–2 minutes until mixture is smooth and shiny.

Pour the mixture into the prepared tins and bake for the time specified for the size of tin used. The cake is done when the edges come away from the tin. Loosen the edges of the cake and turn out onto a wire rack to cool.

QUICK CAKE MIX: SIZE 2
360 g self-raising flour
300 g castor sugar
5 ml salt
125 g butter/margarine (soft or cut into blocks)
2 eggs
200 ml milk
5 ml vanilla essence

Preheat the oven to 180°C and spray the cake tins with non-stick baking spray or butter the tins and sprinkle with flour, shaking out the excess. Place all the ingredients in a mixing bowl and mix, first with a wooden spoon and then with a hand-mixer for 1–2 minutes until mixture is smooth and shiny.

Pour the mixture into the prepared tins and bake for the time specified for the size of tin used. The cake is done when the edges come away from the tin. Loosen the edges of the cake and turn out onto a wire rack to cool.

CHOCOLATE CAKE OR CUP CAKES
For chocolate cake or cup cakes, add 40 g of cocoa for size 1 and 50 g for size 2.

PASTRY CASES

These can be made days in advance. They keep very well for up to a month in an airtight container but can also be frozen. Use the leftover egg whites for meringues, an ever-popular treat at children's parties. This recipe is enough for 10 dozen pastry cases.

240 g cake flour
120 g self-raising flour
120 g cornflour
250 g chilled butter
2 egg yolks
190 ml ice water

Preheat the oven to 180°C and spray patty-pans with non-stick baking spray. Sift the dry ingredients together and rub the butter into the flour mixture until it resembles fine breadcrumbs.

Mix together the yolks and iced water, add to the flour mixture and mix to form dough.

Roll dough out thinly and, using a cookie cutter, cut out circles large enough to fit into a patty-pan. Place dough circles into the pans and prick with a fork.

Bake for 15–18 minutes until golden brown.

MERINGUES

Meringues are favourites at any party. They can be baked in different shapes and then decorated with sweets to resemble animals, insects, toadstools, ghosts, nests and so on. Once they have been baked, sweets can be attached with butter-* or royal icing* or they can be sprinkled with hundreds and thousands or chocolate vermicelli just before baking. Use the leftover egg yolk to make pastry cases*.

2 egg whites
1 ml cream of tartar
pinch of salt
100 g castor sugar
1 ml vanilla essence
food colouring (optional)

Preheat oven to 120°C. Beat egg whites until mixture holds its shape. Add cream of tartar and salt and continue beating until the meringue is stiff, but not dry.

Add the sugar gradually, about 25 ml at a time, beating until dissolved.

Fold in the vanilla with the last 25 ml sugar. Add colouring, if required.

Line a baking sheet with baking paper. Spoon the meringue mixture onto the sheet, shaping them with two spoons, a piping bag, or a large icing tube.

Bake for 1 hour, switch off the oven and leave meringues for another hour to dry out. If desired, sandwich meringues together with whipped cream.

ROYAL ICING

This icing hardens as it dries, making it ideal for sticking biscuits together and for making decorations. You have to work fast, as it hardens very quickly. If you're not going to use it for a while, cover with a damp cloth and place in the refrigerator.

2 egg whites
6 drops lemon juice
350 g icing sugar, sifted
flavouring and colouring

Whisk egg whites with lemon juice until foamy. Add the icing sugar 15 ml at a time, beating until the mixture is thick and forms peaks.

Flavour and colour as required. Makes about 650 ml, enough to ice one large cake.

BUTTER ICING

Butter icing is ideally used to cover and decorate the tops and sides of cakes or cup cakes. Use it as a filling between the layers of a cake or to assemble pieces of cake.

100 g butter or margarine
225–250 g icing sugar
dash of milk
flavouring and colouring

Cream butter or margarine and icing sugar well. Add a small amount of milk to form a soft mixture. (Do not add too much milk as this will make it runny, and you will have to add more icing sugar.) Flavour and colour as desired.

Due to the colour of butter/margarine, this icing will have a creamy colour. If you require white icing for your theme, rather use royal icing.

Sufficient to top a 20 cm cake.

MARSHMALLOW PASTE

This paste can be shaped to form all kinds of edible decorations.

15 g white marshmallows
100 g icing sugar, sifted
food colouring
cornflour

Using your fingers, mix the marshmallows and icing sugar to a firm, elastic paste.

Colour and shape as required, using the cornflour to prevent the paste from sticking to your fingers.

COLOURED DESICCATED COCONUT

Coloured coconut makes an interesting background on which to place cakes and can be used in different ways to decorate the cake itself.

Place any amount of coconut in a mixing bowl. Dilute food colouring with a little water, sprinkle over the coconut and mix well with a spoon or fork.

Spread out on a baking sheet to dry. Green coconut is ideal to simulate grass, while blue or red around a cake creates an interesting effect.

CAKES FOR PRE-TEENS

UPSIDE-DOWN PINEAPPLE CAKE
80 g butter or margarine
150 g brown sugar
1 x 450 g can pineapple rings
125 g butter or margarine
100 g sugar
2 eggs
260 g cake flour
10 ml baking powder
pinch of salt
250 ml pineapple juice
red glace cherries to decorate

Preheat the oven to 180°C and grease a deep 22 cm round cake tin. Cream 80 g of butter or margarine and brown sugar well and spread over the base and sides of the cake tin. Drain the pineapple rings and arrange them on top of the sugar mixture.

Cream 125 g butter and 100 g sugar well. Add eggs one at a time, beating well after each addition. Sift the flour, baking powder and salt and add alternately with the pineapple juice to the creamed mixture. Blend lightly.

Pour the mixture over the pineapples and bake for 1 hour. Remove from oven and turn out on serving plate.

Place a glacé cherry in the centre of each pineapple ring.

COCONUT CAKE
125 g butter or margarine
100 g castor sugar
3 eggs, separated
5 ml vanilla essence
130 g cake flour
10 ml baking powder
125 ml milk
100 g sugar
75 g desiccated coconut

Preheat the oven to 160°C and grease and line a deep, 20 cm round cake tin.

Cream the butter or margarine with 100 g castor sugar. Gradually add the egg yolks and vanilla and beat well.

Sift flour and baking powder and add alternately with the milk to the creamed mixture.

Mix well, then pour into the prepared cake tin.

Whisk the egg whites until soft peaks form. Gradually add the 100 g sugar and beat until stiff. Fold in the coconut, mixing gently.

Spoon the coconut mixture onto the cake mixture and bake for 50–60 minutes.

ORANGE CAKE
250 g butter or margarine
250 g castor sugar
3 eggs
250 g cake flour
10 ml baking powder
pinch of salt
62,5 ml milk

SAUCE
50 ml lemon juice
125 ml orange juice
100 g sugar

Preheat the oven to 180°C, grease a ring pan or spring-form tin and line with greaseproof paper.

Cream butter or margarine and castor sugar until light and fluffy. Add eggs one at a time, beating well after each addition.

Sift dry ingredients and fold into egg mixture (mixture will be fairly stiff). If the mixture is too stiff, add a little milk.

Spoon into the cake tin and bake for about 35 minutes or until a skewer inserted in the centre comes out clean. Meanwhile, make the sauce by mixing the lemon and orange juices with the sugar. Stir over low heat until sugar has dissolved.

Leave cake to stand for about 5 minutes after removing from the oven. Prick holes in it so that the sauce will be absorbed and carefully spoon the sauce over. Leave to cool completely before turning out onto a serving plate.

Food allergies

Children with food allergies may feel that they are different from their friends, which makes it important not to keep them away from parties. Rather try to ensure that provision is made for the child with the allergy. If your child is invited to a party, ask the hostess if it would be okay for the child to bring his own snacks. Ensure that the child knows what he is allowed to eat and what not; also inform the hostess. If you know that children with allergies will attend your child's party, make an extra effort to prepare food which can be enjoyed by all the kids. Always provide a variety of savoury snacks, such as meatballs and cheese snacks, to ensure that diabetic children will have enough to eat. Fruit is a healthy alternative to sweets.

MILK-/DAIRY ALLERGY

The main function of milk in baking is to provide fluid. It can be substituted with soya milk, fruit juice, water or rooibos tea. The texture will be very similar to when milk is used. Substitute one cup of milk with one cup fluid. Butter can be replaced with margarine made from vegetable oils. Ensure that the packaging says *margarine* and not *spread,* as most spreads are not suitable for baking.

WHEAT/GLUTEN ALLERGY

Wheat and gluten in recipes contribute to the elasticity and viscosity of the dough, as well as the way in which the different ingredients bind. Kneading dough forms gluten, which gives it a well-risen and fine texture, as in bread.

When you bake a cake the dough should normally not be handled a lot, as the texture needs to be crumbly. If you use a substitute for cake flour in a recipe, the cake will probably rise less and have a more doughy texture. This can be improved by sifting the flour to allow more air into the mixture. Substitute 250 ml cake flour in any recipe with one of the following:

- 220 ml rice flour or
- 150 ml potato flour or
- 250 ml soya flour plus 60 ml potato flour or
- 250 ml cornflour

EGG ALLERGIES

Eggs are used in dough and batter to enclose air, allowing it to rise well. When batter does not include egg, the amount of raising agent used should be increased. Try one of the following combinations as a substitute for eggs in a recipe (you can substitute up to three eggs). Substitute one egg with:

- 5 ml baking powder, 15 ml fluids, 15 ml vinegar or
- 5 ml dry yeast, dissolved in 62,5 ml warm water or
- 20 ml water, 20 ml oil, 5 ml baking powder
- 1 packet of gelatine dissolved in 30 ml warm water

DIABETICS

Diabetics cannot eat food with a high sugar content and party cakes usually have a very high sugar content. People who have to avoid sugar can usually eat food containing fructose instead of sucrose. Normal cane sugar contains sucrose, but fructose is found in the natural sugar of fruit, which does not need insulin to be digested by the body.

Replace cane sugar in a recipe with fructose powder or artificial sweeteners in powder or liquid form. Fructose is twice as sweet as cane sugar. Some artificial sweeteners can be 200 to 2 000 times sweeter than sugar. Do not use more than the quantities to be used in adapted recipes. Too much sugar substitute will definitely spoil the taste of your baking. Fructose also causes severe browning of batter when baked. Some artificial sweeteners are not suitable for baking, as the heat destroys the sweet taste. Ensure that the one you choose is suitable. Natreen usually works well.

RECIPES

DOUBLE LAYER BIRTHDAY CAKE
This cake is milk and egg free.

750 ml cake flour
440 ml sugar
300 ml water
125 ml margarine
45 ml water, 45 ml oil, 10 ml
baking powder mixed
15 ml baking powder
5 ml salt
5 ml vanilla essence

Preheat oven to 180°C. Grease two cake tins with margarine or spray with non-stick baking spray.

Mix all the ingredients in a large bowl and beat for approximately 4 minutes at a high speed. Pour the batter into two cake tins and bake for 40 to 50 minutes.

Allow to stand in the tins for 10 minutes before turning out onto a wire rack to cool. Decorate the cake once completely cooled.

WHEAT-FREE CHOCOLATE BROWNIES
500 ml oatmeal
180 ml cocoa
250 ml icing sugar
pinch of salt
2,5 ml baking powder
250 ml margarine
5 ml vanilla essence
1 small egg

Preheat oven to 150°C. Mix all the ingredients thoroughly until dough forms. Refrigerate the dough for at least 1 hour. Roll out and cut into squares. Place the squares onto a baking sheet and prick with a fork. Bake for 25 minutes.

GLUTEN FREE APPLE CAKE
125 ml margarine
250 ml honey
20 ml water
20 ml oil
1 egg
5 ml vanilla essence
550 ml cornflour
5 ml baking powder
10 ml cinnamon
250 ml seedless raisins (optional)
2,5 ml salt
250 ml unsweetened apple sauce

Preheat oven to 180°C. Grease a rectangular cake tin and sprinkle with flour, or spray with non-stick baking spray. Cream margarine and slowly add the honey. Beat until light and fluffy. Add the egg and vanilla and beat thoroughly.

Mix the dry ingredients in a bowl. Add the mixture and the apple sauce alternately to the honey mixture and beat well. Add the raisins and pour batter into the tin. Bake for 35 minutes and turn out onto wire rack to cool.

CHOCOLATE CAKE FOR DIABETICS
30 g cocoa
150 ml boiling water
125 g margarine
200 g fructose
2 egg yolks
130 g whole wheat flour
120 g cake flour
5 ml cream of tartar
5 ml bicarbonate of soda
pinch of salt
10 ml vanilla
150 ml plain yoghurt
4 egg whites, beaten

Preheat oven to 180°C. Grease a 23 cm round cake tin with margarine or spray with non-stick baking spray.

Mix cocoa with boiling water until smooth and leave to cool. Cream the margarine and fructose. Add the egg yolks and cocoa mixture to creamed margarine and stir well.

Mix the flour, cream of tartar, bicarbonate of soda, baking powder and salt. Add the dry ingredients and yoghurt alternately to the creamed mixture. Mix well after each addition.

Fold the beaten egg whites into the mixture. Pour mixture into cake tins and bake for 25–35 minutes. Turn out onto wire rack. Allow to cool completely before decorating.

ICING
2 slabs of dark chocolate for diabetics; 1 slab white chocolate for diabetics

Melt the chocolate over simmering water and pour over the cake.

(Recipe adapted from *Cooking the diabetic way* by Hilda Lategan e.a., Tafelberg 2001.)

Some of the recipes given here can be found on the following websites:
http://www.foodallergy.org
http://www.skyisland.com

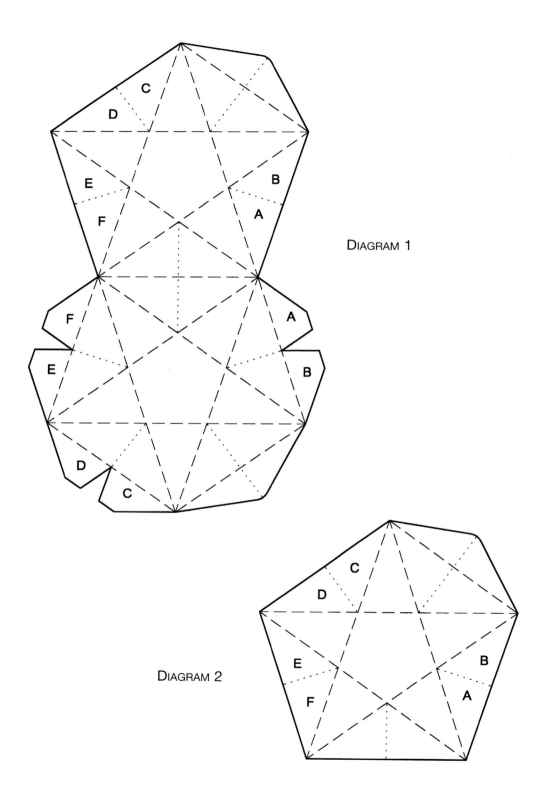

DIAGRAM 1

DIAGRAM 2

STAR BOX

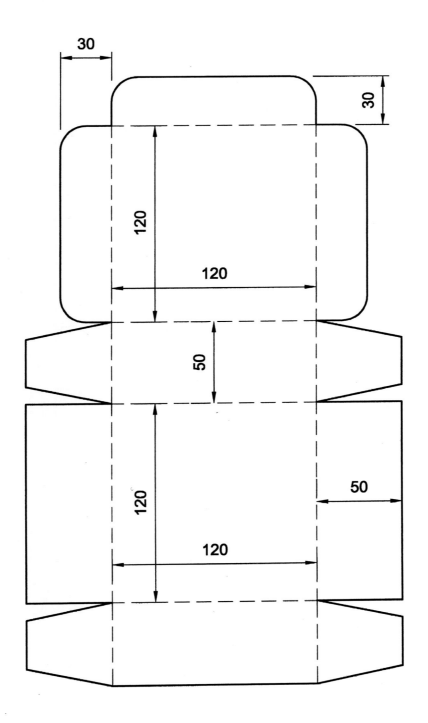

ANIMAL FACE BOXES

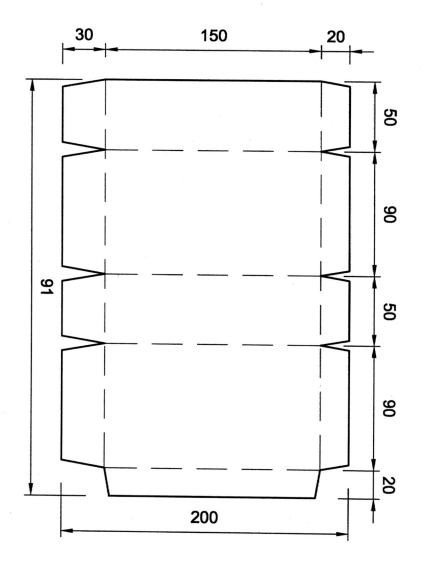

PIRATE'S BAG